On the Move in Wales 1

1 Sports crossword

a Fill in the crossword. The photos can help you.

Crossword answers:
- 1 Down: HOCKEY
- 2 Down: RUGBY
- 3 Down: ATHLETICS
- 4 Down: BADMINTON
- 5 Across: IN-LINE SKATING
- 6 Across: PE
- 7 Down: SKIING
- 8 Across: CRICKET
- 9 Across: SWIMMING
- 10 Across: GOLF

→ Across

5 You need special shoes for this. You can do it in parks and on pavements
6 The word for sport when you do it at school.
8 This game with a ball is very popular in Britain, India and Australia, but not in Germany or the USA.
9 In the summer you can do it in a lake. In the winter you have to go inside.
10 You hit a little ball into a hole and you walk a lot.

↓ Down

1 You can play this game on ice or on grass.
2 A lot of teams in Wales play this sport. The ball is like an egg, but bigger.
3 This includes different activities – you run, jump and throw.
4 2 or 4 people can play. It's like tennis, but you don't use a ball.
7 For this you need snow and hills or mountains.

b **Now you and a partner**

Write some sentences about a sport or a hobby. Don't write the name! Think about these questions:

What do you need for this activity?
Do you do it in a team?
What do you do?
Where do you do it?
Which countries are especially good at this?

Can your partner guess what it is?

1

2 Revision: Julia and her dad choose a new school

Julia's family is moving to Wales. Complete the story. Use verbs from the box in the *simple past*.

> ask • choose • go
> leave • look • move
> phone • read
> send • ~~sit~~ • write

In May Julia's father _sat_ down and _wrote_ to some schools for information. Early in June all the schools _send_ their brochures. Julia and her dad _read_ them carefully and _chose_ Aberaeron. The next day Julia's dad _phoned_ the school and _asked_ for a place. In July they _left_ London and _moved_ to Wales. On their first day in the new flat, they _went_ and _looked_ at the school for the first time.

TIP

Remember irregular verbs like this:

'Cat' verbs say 'm i a u':
sw<u>i</u>m, sw<u>a</u>m, sw<u>u</u>m

'Echo' verbs:
w<u>i</u>n, w<u>o</u>n, w<u>o</u>n

'Sandwich' verbs:
c<u>o</u>me, c<u>a</u>me, c<u>o</u>me

'Chicken' verbs:
p<u>u</u>t, p<u>u</u>t, p<u>u</u>t

'Lost letter' verbs:
me<u>e</u>t, met, met

3 Revision: Julia's list

a Julia has got a big list of jobs. What has she already done? What hasn't she done yet?

- clean the kitchen cupboard ✓
- wash the kitchen floor ✗
- put my pens and pencils in my desk ✓
- check my homework ✗
- do my music practice ✗
- write to Susie in Bangor ✓

1 She has already _cleaned the kitchen cupboard_
2 She hasn't _washed the kitchen floor yet_
3 She has _already put her pens and pencils in her desk_
4 _She hasn't checked her homework yet_
5 _She hasn't done her musik practise yet_
6 _She has already written to Susie in Bangor_

b What jobs have you already done today? What haven't you done yet? Write two sentences.

_____

_____

p. 10

1

4 Are you an exciting person?

a Write about things you've done. You don't have to tell the truth all the time. Three sentences should be false! Here are some verbs you can use:

> meet • read • see
> win • write

1 I've been to _____.
2 I've _____.
3 I've _____.
4 _____
5 _____
6 _____

b **Now you and a partner**
Ask your partner questions and find out which sentences are true. Talk like this:

A Have you really been to England?
B Yes, I have. I went there on holiday two years ago.
A Have you really won a prize on a TV show?
B No, of course I haven't!

c Write about what you really have done – and when you did it.
Example: *I really have been to America. I went there last year.*

1 _____
2 _____
3 _____

5 A message about sport

Fill in the crossword.

1 They tell you what you must and mustn't do.
2 Don't work too hard. You need to … sometimes.
3 We won. The … was 6:0.
4 Do you like sport? You should join a … .
5 I have to go to … every Thursday evening.
6 'And here are the football … .'
7 Amy is always … . I think she trains too much.
8 It can be a vehicle, or a sports trainer.
9 There are 15 people in a rugby … .
10 In football you score a … .
11 In rugby you score a … .
12 "We are the … !"

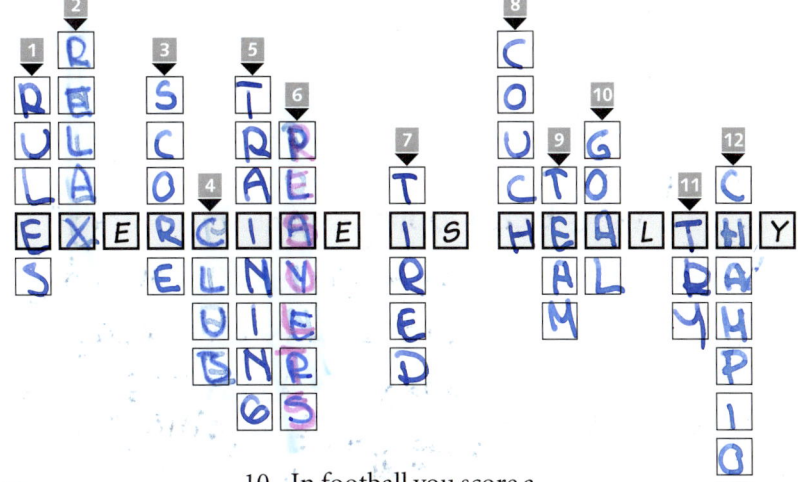

p. 10

6 How long have they been at this school?

Put in *for* or *since*.

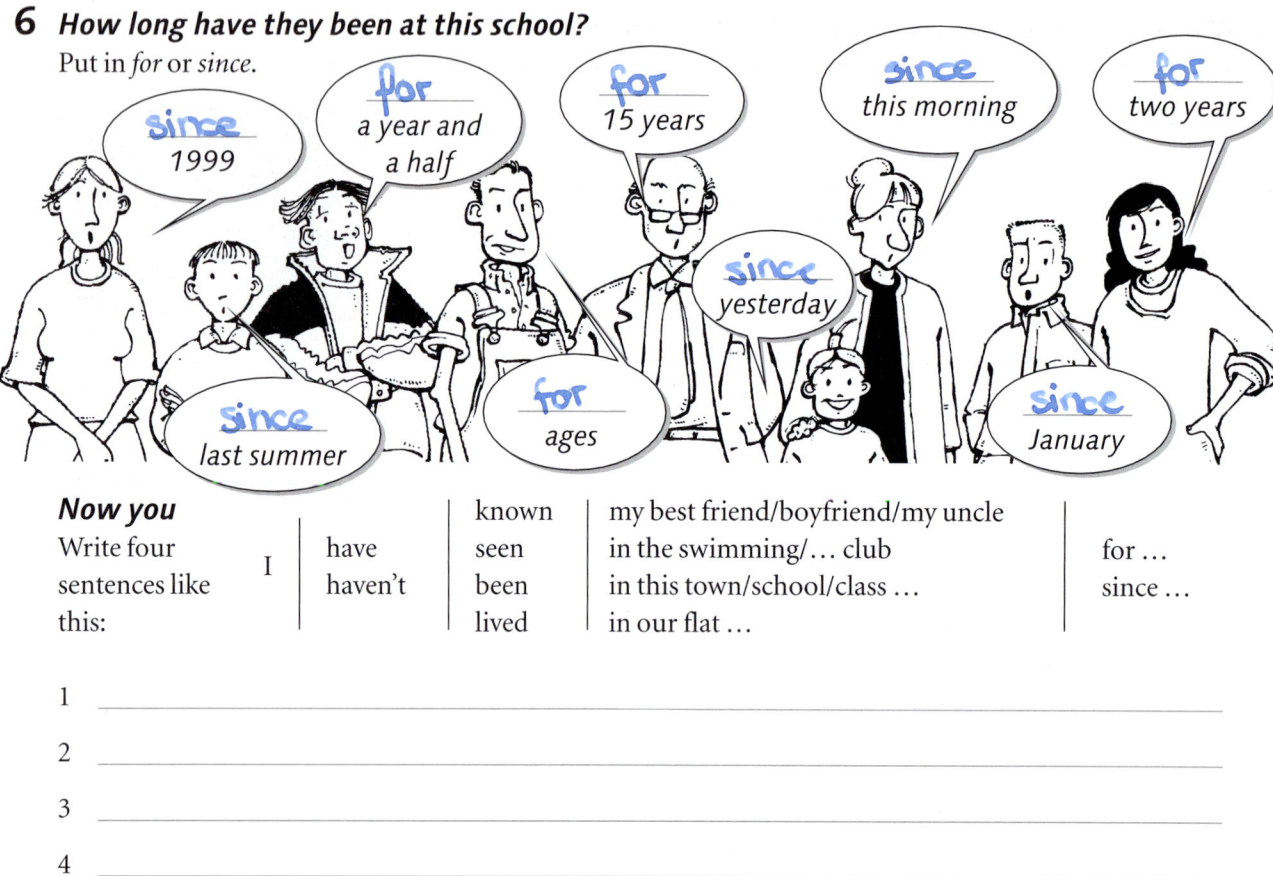

speech bubbles: since 1999 / for a year and a half / for 15 years / since this morning / for two years / since last summer / since yesterday / for ages / since January

Now you
Write four sentences like this:

| | I | have / haven't | known / seen / been / lived | my best friend/boyfriend/my uncle in the swimming/… club in this town/school/class … in our flat … | for … since … |

1 _____
2 _____
3 _____
4 _____

7 How long have you been doing it?

Complete the sentences with the *present perfect progressive* and *for* or *since*.

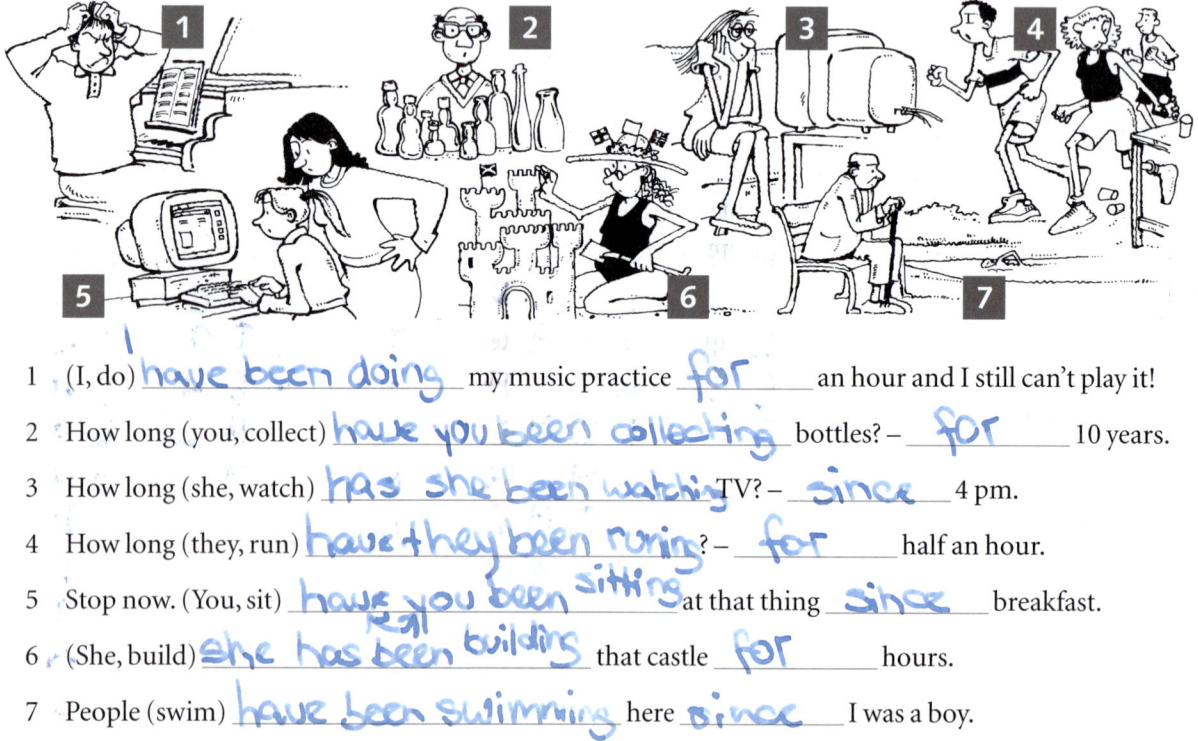

1 (I, do) **have been doing** my music practice **for** an hour and I still can't play it!
2 How long (you, collect) **have you been collecting** bottles? – **for** 10 years.
3 How long (she, watch) **has she been watching** TV? – **since** 4 pm.
4 How long (they, run) **have they been runing**? – **for** half an hour.
5 Stop now. (You, sit) **have you been sitting** at that thing **since** breakfast.
6 (She, build) **she has been building** that castle **for** hours.
7 People (swim) **have been swimming** here **since** I was a boy.

8 Mediation: What would you ask Wayne Rooney?

a Imagine you have a chance to meet Wayne Rooney and ask him some questions. What would you say?

Du möchtest wissen:

1 … wie lange er schon bei Manchester United spielt.

_____

2 … wann er geboren wurde.

_____

3 … wo er zur Schule ging.

_____

4 … für welche Mannschaft er vor Manchester United gespielt hat.

_____

5 Bei der EM 2004 hat er gegen die Schweiz gespielt – wie viele Tore hat er geschossen?

At Euro 2004 _____

_____

b Try and find the answers to your questions on the Internet.

1 _____
2 _____
3 _____
4 _____
5 _____

9 What do you think about sport?

Do you like sport – or do you hate it? How much sport do you do? Do you do different sports in winter and summer? Are you interested in other things?

What about the rest of your class? Make a questionnaire with ten questions. Use the ideas above or your own ideas. Ask ten people in your class the questions and write a short text with the results.

10 % of the people I asked think that _____

_____

_____

_____

1

Working with the text "The Race"

10 *Questions*

Mr Evans is telling a friend about David's weekend. Write the friend's questions.

1 Who _____ ? They played Llandysul.
2 _____ ? The score was 24:17.
3 _____ ? Yes, David played really well.
4 _____ ? Tom Porter won the cycle race.
5 _____ ? Yes, some people were surprised.
6 _____ ? Because he stopped and helped Aled.

11 *Listening to the text*

Listen to the radio interview with Aled Jones. Then answer the following questions.

1 Why did Aled fall after the 55-kilometre checkpoint? *He lost control over his bike*
2 What did David do when he saw that Aled was hurt? *He stopped and rode back*
3 What were Aled's first words to David after he fell? *I think my leg is broken*
4 What did Aled say when David told him that he was going to wait for an ambulance?
"Get back on your bike!" Win for us
5 Why was Aled sorry that David didn't win?
Aled wanted to beat the champion next year

12 *Beyond the text*

Write about a sports event.
Answer the questions in a paragraph.

- What event do you remember?
- Did you play in it or did you watch it?
- How did you feel when it started?
- Did your team start well or badly?
- What happened after that?
- At the end, what was the score and how did you feel?

I remember the volleyball match between pupils and teachers at the end of the summer term last year.

p. 18

TOPIC 1

13 Mediation: On holiday in Wales

Your family is staying on a farm in the Gwaun Valley in Wales. On your first day your mother is talking to the farmer's wife, Mrs Thomas. Your mother doesn't speak much English, so you need to help them.

Mrs Thomas	Bore da – good morning. Did you sleep well? Is everything all right?
Mother	Good morning. (*To you*) Ich habe sie sonst gar nicht verstanden. Was hat sie denn gesagt?
You	Sie hat nur gefragt, ob wir gut geschlafen haben & ob alles ok ist
Mother	Yes, thank you. Everything is very nice. (*To you*) Ach, ich wollte Mrs Thomas fragen, wo der nächste Supermarkt ist und ob sie ein gutes Restaurant hier in der Nähe kennt.
You	My mother would like to know where the nearest supermarket is next to here & if you now a good restaurant here?
Mrs Thomas	Yes, the nearest supermarket is just outside Fishguard, about three miles from here. And there's a good Italian restaurant in Newport, to the north of here. It's opposite the castle. It's called Gino's. The fish there is very good.
You	Thank you. Sie sagt der nächste supermarkt ist 3 meilen entfernt in Fishguard und es gibt ein guter Italienisches restaurant nördlich von dort in Newport. Es heißt Gino's und der Fisch dort schmeckt sehr gut (gegenüber Schloss)
Mother	Thank you very much. (*To you*) Und vielleicht kann sie uns auch noch einen schönen Strand empfehlen?
You	Mrs Thomas, do you now a nice beach? can you tell us about a nice beach here?
Mrs Thomas	Oh yes, there are lots, but my favourite is at Mwnt¹, just north of Cardigan. It's in a small bay and very beautiful. It's best to go there early in the day, because parking is a bit of a problem.
You	Sie sagt, es gibt viele, aber ihr Lieblingsstrand ist Mwnt nördlich von Cardigan. Es ist klein sehr schön und hat eine Bucht. Am besten wir gehen in der Früh dort hin, weil Parken ein kleines Problem ist
Mother	Mrs Thomas kennt sich ja gut hier aus. Frag sie doch mal, wie lange sie hier schon wohnt.
You	My mother would like to know how long have you been living here?
Mrs Thomas	Oh, let me think. I came here in 1977, when I got married. I lived in Bangor, in the North. That's where I met Morgan, my husband.
You	Sie kam 1977 hier her als sie heiratete. Sie lebte in norden in Bangor, dort traf sie ihren mann Morgan.
	(*To Mrs Thomas*) Thank you very much, Mrs Thomas.
Mrs Thomas	Glad to help you. Let's hope the weather stays fine for you.

¹Mwnt [mʊnt]

1 NOW YOU CAN ...

14 **... talk about sport**
How do you say these things in English?

1 Frage jemanden, welche Sportart in seiner/ihrer Klasse beliebt ist.

2 Sage, dass bei den Mädchen Schwimmen sehr beliebt ist.

3 Sage, dass die Jungen meinen, dass Fußball mehr Spaß macht.

4 Sage, dass du eine gute Nachricht hast. Deine Mannschaft hat 3:1 gewonnen.

5 Sage, dass du zu viel Zeit beim Sport verbringst.

6 Sage, dass das Quatsch ist. Sport ist gesund.

15 **... use the right preposition**
Use the words in the balls.

1 Can you listen _____ the phone please? I'm going out _____ the dog. I'll be back _____ half an hour.

2 Your attitude _____ your work has changed. You were usually so careful _____ your homework, but this is full _____ mistakes.

3 David and Emma have lots _____ common. Both _____ them look forward _____ going cycling together.

4 What do you want _____ your birthday? – Money! Will you spend it _____ a new bike? – Yes, and I'll take care _____ it better than the old one.

5 You must be here _____ ten o'clock. We'll wait _____ 10.10, but then we'll go _____ you.

16 **... plan a tour for some visitors**
Imagine you have a class of English visitors at your school. Work in a group and choose the sights you want to show them. Each pupil writes a short text on a separate piece of paper (10 x 15 cm) about one or two of the sights. Then put all the texts together to make your own tourist brochure.

Role-play Visitors and hosts (*Gastgeber*) read the leaflet together and plan a tour of your area.

REVISION BOOK 2 Fitness check

How fit are you in English? How much can you remember from the last two years? Do these exercises and check. The ▶ boxes can help you.

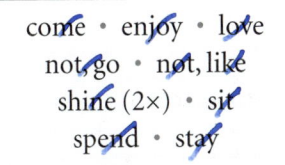

1 Letters to Lizzy

The twins Zak and Zoe have written letters to their friend Lizzy. Complete the gaps in the letters. Use the right forms of the verbs in the boxes.

Dear Lizzy,

I ~~enjoyed~~ *am enjoying* our holiday in Spain very much. We ~~stay~~ *come* here every year and I *love* it. We always ~~come~~ *stay* at the Hotel Playa. It's great in Spain because the sun *shines* every day. It *shines* now and I ~~stay~~ *sitting* by the pool. We ~~didn't go~~ ~~don't going~~ to the beach at midday — it's too hot, especially for Zak. He ~~doesn't~~ ~~don't likes~~ the sun. He *sit* a lot of time in his room!

Love, Zoe

come • enjoy • ~~love~~
~~not, go~~ • ~~not, like~~
~~shine (2×)~~ • ~~sit~~
~~spend~~ • ~~stay~~

come • go • ~~feel~~
~~like~~ • ~~love~~
~~not, do~~ • not, sit
~~spend (2×)~~ • swim

Dear Lizzy,

Does your family *go* to boring places on holiday? *Do* you *like* hot weather? I don't! *Do* you *feel* fed up at the moment? I am. We *are spending* our holiday in Spain again this year. We *are spending* every holiday in Spain. We ~~go~~ *come* to the same hotel, and we *don't do* anything new. It's really hot now, so I *not sitting* outside — Zoe *is swimming*. She *loves* it here — I can't understand why.

Love, Zak

> ▶ In English you have to choose between the *simple present* and the *present progressive*:
>
> You use the simple present when you talk about things that **sometimes**, **often** or **never** happen, e.g.
> *He always gets up late at the weekend.*
> Don't forget the 's' with 'he', 'she' and 'it'!
>
> You use the present progressive when something is happening **now**, e.g.
> *Listen! The baby is crying.*
> You often use this tense with words like 'now' and 'at the moment'.

REVISION BOOK 2 Fitness check

2 An interview
These were the answers. What were the questions?

1 Where _____ when you were a child? • I lived in Haiti until I was 7 then I moved to the USA.

2 Who _____ ? • My mother taught me. She's a great singer.

3 Where _____ ? • I met them at school. All the other members of the band are old school friends.

4 How often _____ ? • We practised all the time.

5 Who _____ ? • We all chose it. Don't you think it's a great name for a band?

6 Who _____ ? • My parents helped me at the start – and my friends of course.

7 When _____ ? • Our first CD appeared in 1994.

8 When _____ ? • We became really famous in 1995 when our second CD came out.

> Some of these are subject questions and some are object questions. Do you remember the difference?
>
> *Willst du wissen, wer's gemacht, sind „do/does/did" nicht angebracht. Willst du wissen, Wem? oder Wen?, dann müssen „do/does/did" dort stehn.*

3 A perfect crossword

a Read the clues and complete the crossword.

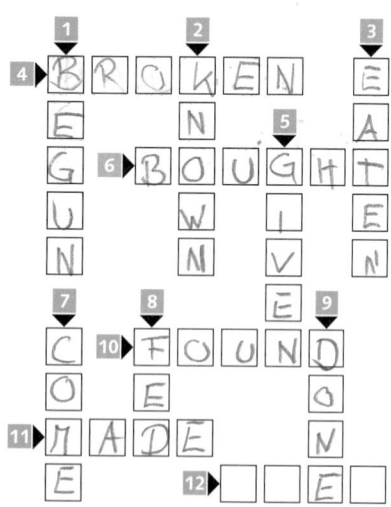

1 The new term has ... . The holidays have finished.
2 How long have you ... your best friend? – I met her two years ago.
3 The dog hasn't ... her food. She must be ill.
4 I can't play football – I've ... my leg.
5 The teacher has ... us a lot of homework. I'm going to start it now.
6 Have you ... a new CD? Can I borrow it?
7 Dad hasn't ... home yet.
8 Have you ... the cat? It looks hungry.
9 Have you ... your homework yet?
10 The Smiths lost their cat last week and they haven't ... it yet.
11 Have you ever ... bread? It's easy to make.
12 Mum has ... home and now she's gone again.

b Make a table like this in your exercise book. Write down all three forms of the verbs in the crossword.

Infinitive	Simple past	Past participle
break	broke	broken
buy	...	...

REVISION BOOK 2 Fitness check

4 Present perfect or simple past
How do you say these things in English?

1 Frage deine Freundin / deinen Freund, wie lange sie/er schon hier ist.
   How long have you been here?

2 Sage, dass du schon seit langem hier bist.
   I've been here for a long time
   I'm a very long time here

3 Frage, wann er/sie gekommen ist.
   come here
   I arrived at 6 o'clock

4 Sage, dass du um sechs Uhr angekommen bist.

5 Frage, ob er/sie schon die Karten gekauft hat.
   Have you already bough the tickets

6 Sage nein, weil du nicht genug Geld hattest.
   No, I didn't I've not enough money

7 Frage, ob er/sie schon in diesem Kino war.
   Have you ever been to cinema?

8 Sage, dass du letzte Woche hier warst und einen 'Star Wars'-Film gesehen hast.
   I was last week here and watched "Star Wars".

> Be careful. The German *Perfekt* can be *simple past* or *present perfect*.
> e.g. *Ich habe ein Buch gekauft.*
> = I've **bought** a book.
> But *Ich habe gestern ein Buch gekauft.*
> = I **bought** a book yesterday.

Do you want to say <u>when</u> something happened? Use the simple past with time expressions like <u>yesterday, two days ago, last week ...</u>

With the present perfect, you often use words like this: <u>just, already, never, before, not ... yet</u>

5 What can they do?
A German girl, Leonie, is coming to stay with Emma. What can they do? Finish the sentences.

1 If Leonie likes shopping, *they can go to town* .
2 If she's interested in old places, _____.
3 If the weather is hot, _____.
4 If the weather is bad, _____.
5 If Leonie likes cycling, _____.
6 If Leonie doesn't understand something in English, _____.
7 If she's interested in Welsh, _____.

11

REVISION BOOK 2 Fitness check

6 Thinking about the future
Complete the sentences. Use the *going to-*future or the *will-*future.

 I think I (get) __will get__ a job in a bank when I leave school.
I don't think I (work) __will work__ in a factory.

(you, stay) __Do you gonna stay__ at home this summer?
– No, we (go) __are going to go__ to France.

 I (not, go out) __'m not going to go out__ tonight. Dad (cook) __is going to cook__ a special meal because it's Mum's birthday.

Maybe I (buy) __will buy__ a motorbike when I'm old enough. I'm sure I (not, buy) __'m not going to by__ a car.

 What (you, do) __will you do__ this afternoon?
– I (look) __'m going to look for__ at sports shoes in town.

> You use the *will-*future for predictions – in German 'Vorhersagen und Vermutungen'. You use the *going to-*future when you are talking about a plan.
>
> *Will*' often goes with expressions like *I think, I'm sure, maybe ...*

7 Better or worse?
Complete the sentences.

1 Do you think the weather will be (*besser*) _____ tomorrow?

2 I hope so. Today was (*der schlimmste*) _____ day we've had for ages.

3 I think yesterday was (*viel schlimmer*) _____ .

4 Can you work a bit (*schneller*) _____ ? I want to finish this exercise
  (*so schnell wie*) _____ I can.

5 You read that really (*gut*) _____ . Can you read it again, but this time read a bit
  (*langsamer*) _____ .

London 2

1 Words in words

a You can make lot of words with the letters in *Thames River Tours*, e.g. *ours, more, tourists, …* . How many more words can you find in three minutes? (Your words should have three or more letters.)

maths, sea, mum, roam, three, hair, theater, were, she, have, arms, meet, team, same, castes, meat, house, time, met,

b Write a story in class: Start a story using a word from your list in a sentence. The next pupil continues the story with a word from his/her list, and so on.

2 A postcard from London

a This postcard has been in the rain and is hard to read. Complete the postcard. Pages 22–23 and page 149 of your pupil's book can help you.

> **TIP**
> In English nouns like *queen* or *tower* do not usually start with a capital letter. But they do when we are talking about one special queen or tower – for example, *Queen Elizabeth* or the *Tower of London*.

Dear David

Hi! Well, here we are in L_ondon_, and we've seen lots. On Monday we went to the _Tower of Lon_don and saw the _Cro_wn Je_wles_ there. Then we saw a Shakespeare play at the G_loube_ Th_eatre_. Yesterday we saw the _Londo_n Du_ngeon_: scary! And this morning we went on a boat trip on the _Thimes_ s. We started from near the _hous_es of _Parlame_nt, and we saw a lot of interesting places from the boat. Oh, no! It's starting to rain!

Love, Brigitta

David He
24600 SW 119
Miami
FL 33177
USA

Now you and a partner

b Copy a paragraph from a text from Unit 1 of your pupil's book. Leave out one or two words in each sentence and put them in a box (not in the same order!). Swap paragraphs and try to find your partner's words.

pp. 22–23 (p. 149)

3 All about London

Complete the sentences. Use the verbs in the box in the passive – *simple present* or *simple past*.

> bring • build • find • hurt
> sell • speak • steal • take • visit

1 There was an accident on the underground yesterday. Several people _____ and two people _____ to hospital in an ambulance.

2 Madame Tussaud's _____ by two million people every year.

3 Do you know how many languages _____ in London?

4 If you want a cheap ticket to the theatre, go to the ticket office just before the play starts. Sometimes tickets _____ at cheap prices.

5 This museum sounds exciting. It says in the brochure: "In the museum's Darwin Centre new scientific discoveries _____ to life."

6 Ask the guides anything you like: When _____ this building _____? Who was born here? They know everything.

7 My friend's bag _____ from his hotel room. It _____ later, but the thieves had taken all his money.

4 The school newspaper

a Zak runs the Liddleton School newspaper. Read the interview with him.

Tom   How many people work on the paper?
Zak   About six people do most of the work.
Tom   What do you do first?
Zak   Well, first we need some articles. Different people write them and send them to our office. Then I sit down with a couple of other people and we choose the best ones.
Tom   What about photos?
Zak   We have our own photographers. They take the pictures we need. When it's all ready we have to sell the paper. We sell it in school. Quite a lot of people buy it!

b Finish this report for the school website about Zak's paper. Use the *simple present passive*.

Liddleton School Homepage

THE SCHOOL NEWSPAPER – DID YOU KNOW?

Most of the work _____. First of all, the articles _____. Then the best articles _____. The photos _____. _____. The paper _____. You should buy it too – it's good! Next issue: Tuesday.

---

p. 25/A6

2

5 Revision: London taxi puzzle

a Complete the puzzle.

1 It's the name of the man whose statue is in the middle of Trafalgar Square.
2 It's someone who robs you.
3 It's the clock that you can see near the Houses of Parliament.
4 It's someone who can tell you about the sights.
5 It's a kind of bus that tourists often use.
6 It's something that is sometimes worn by the queen.
7 It's a word that is used for the underground.
8 It's the river that goes through London.
9 The figures that are in Madame Tussaud's are made of this.
10 It's someone who wants to see the sights.

b Look again at the clues in *a*. Which relative pronouns can you leave out?

c Make clues for this puzzle like the ones in *a*.

TIP

Remember: If there's a noun between 'who' or 'that' and the verb, you can leave it out!
It's a kind of bus <u>that</u> tourists often <u>use</u>.
It's a kind of bus tourists often use.

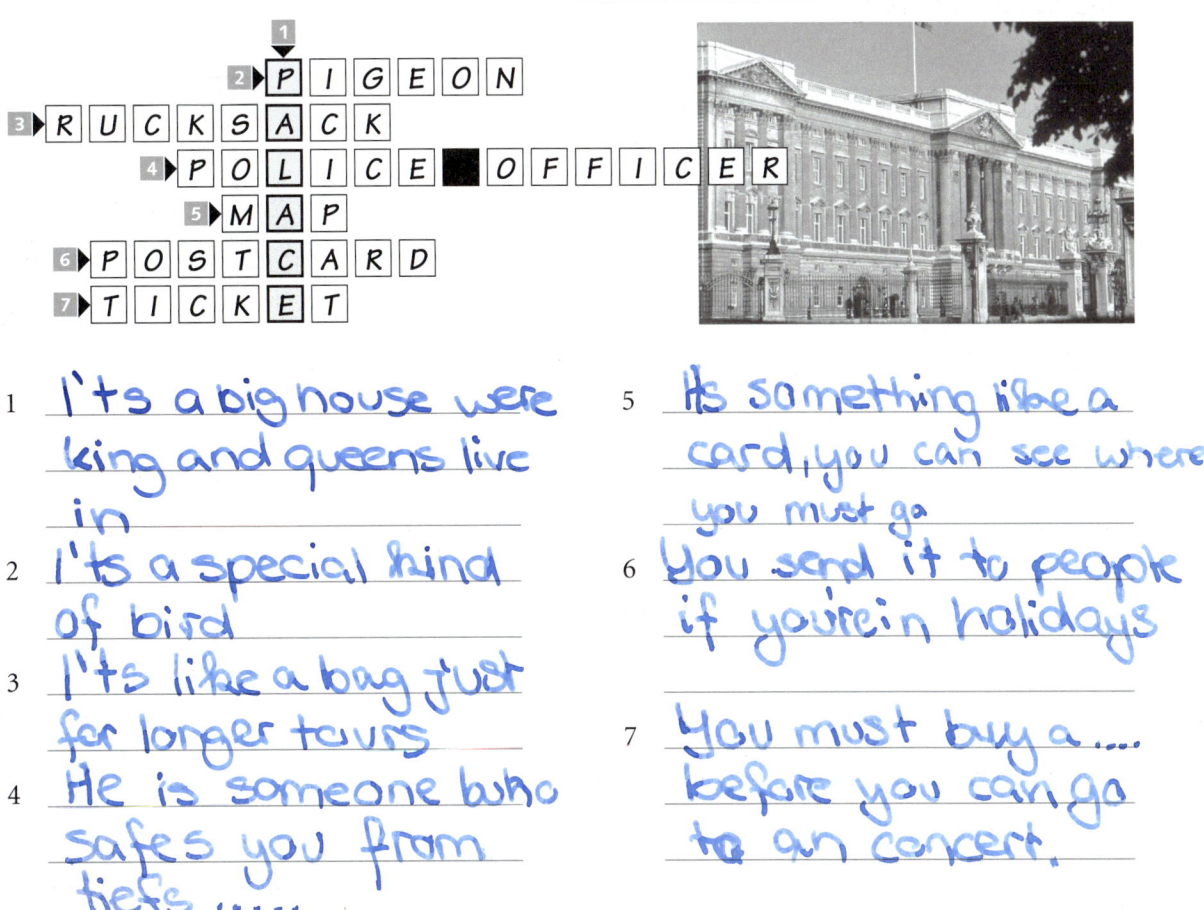

1 It's a big house were king and queens live in
2 It's a special kind of bird
3 It's like a bag just for longer tours
4 He is someone who safes you from tiefs, ...
5 It's something like a card, you can see where you must go
6 You send it to people if you're in holidays
7 You must buy a .... before you can go to an concert.

p. 26

15

6 Revision: Questions, questions

a Ask questions and answer them.

How much How many	TV/watch every day? books/read every month? pocket money/get every week? magazines/buy every month? homework/do every day?	Lots! About … Only a few. About … Only a little. About … None.

1 *How much TV do you* _____ ? _____

2 _____ _____

3 _____ _____

4 _____ _____

5 _____ _____

b Look at your answers. What do you think? Do you watch too much TV/do enough homework, etc.? Write a text about yourself.

_____

_____

_____

_____

_____

_____

_____

7 What should be done?

Finish the sentences to explain these signs. Use the *passive*.

1 Rubbish should _____ .

2 Cars mustn't _____ .

3 Ice creams can't _____ .

4 This can _____ .

5 Bikes should _____ .

p. 27/A10 • p. 28/A15

8 Help the tour guide

A tour guide is telling some tourists all about London. Complete the sentences. You have to choose whether to use the *active* or *passive* form of the verbs in brackets.

Madame Tussaud's (open) __was opened__ in 1835 near to the present museum. It (be) __has been__ very successful ever since and it (visit) __is visited__ by about 2 million people each year.

William I (start) __started__ the Tower of London in 1066. The Crown Jewels (keep) __have been kept__ there for hundreds of years. Two of Henry VIII's wives (put) __were put__ in the Tower of London, where they (execute) __were executed__.

Chinatown (fill) __will be filled__ with people at the weekend because of the Chinese New Year Parade, which (hold) __is held__ every year. Part of the Parade (take place) __took place__ in Trafalgar square this year. But remember: pickpockets (be) __are Sinn!__ at the parade at the weekend. Handbags and purses (keep) __should be kept__ safe at all times. More information on all the sights (find) __could have been found__ in our brochure.

9 When you were a tourist

Write about a trip to a city or another interesting place.

Think about:
- who you went with
- how you travelled
- the sights you visited
- the people you saw
- the place(s) you liked best
- any problems you had

Working with the text "Save the Crown Jewels"

10 *Well done, 101!*
What's the shortest route to save the Crown Jewels? Write the letters A–K in the boxes.

11 *All about London*
On your way round London you should have learned lots of things about London.
Try this quiz. Then scan the text to check your answers.

1 Where can you find the Crown Jewels?
2 Who is on top of the column in Trafalgar Square?
3 How high is the column in Trafalgar Square?
4 What was the name of Shakespeare's theatre?
5 What street did Sherlock Holmes live in?
6 Who was Anne Boleyn?
7 What can you do in Paddington?
8 How many wives did King Henry VIII have?

TOPIC 2

12 Mediation: A trip on the Thames

You are on a boat trip on the Thames with your parents, who do not understand much of the guide's English. Answer their questions.

Guide We are now passing the Tower of London. This is where the Crown Jewels are kept. In the past enemies of the king were sent to the Tower. Many of them died there. The White Tower in the centre is the oldest part. It was built by William I in 1097.

Mother Mei, was sagt er bloß? Ich kann gar nichts verstehen.

You Er sagt, dass wir ___nun am Tower of London vorbeikommen___

Da sind auch ___die Kronjuwelen___.

Früher ___wurden viele Feinde vom König dorthin gesandt.___

Viele ___Menschen, von ihnen starben dort___.

Der älteste Teil heißt „White Tower" und wurde ___von William I 1097 erbaut.___

Guide To your left behind Southwark Bridge you can see the Globe Theatre. It is not the original theatre, but it is like the theatre where Shakespeare's plays were first shown.

Mother Ach, links ist das Theater, wo Shakespeares Stücke aufgeführt wurden.

You Nicht ganz. Es ist nicht ___ein Nachbau nicht das original aber es ist nachgebaut wie als früher noch Stücke vorgeführt würden___

Guide On your right you can see St. Paul's Cathedral. It was built by Sir Christopher Wren in 1711, after the old St. Paul's Cathedral was destroyed in the Fire of London in 1666.

Father Ich kann ihn auch nicht verstehen. Warum spricht er nicht das Englisch, das ich in der Schule gelernt habe?

You Papa, das ist doch so lange her. Er sagt, rechts ___kann man St. Pauls Cathedral schon___

Sie wurde ___1711 von Sir Christoper Wren erbaut davor wurde sie bei einem Brand 1666 zerstört.___

Guide We have just passed under the Millennium Bridge. It was built in 2000 by Sir Norman Foster and is 325 metres long. Our German visitors will remember that Norman Foster also designed the new *Reichstag* in Berlin.

Father Was hat er über den Reichstag gesagt?

You ___Das der der die Millenium Bridge gebaut hat, Sir Norman Forster, auch unseren Reichstag gebaut hat. Außerdem ist die Brücke 325 m lang.___

2 NOW YOU CAN ...

13 ... **talk about travel in English**
How do you say these things in English?

1. Sage, dass du einen Zug zum Flughafen nehmen musst.
2. Schlage jemandem vor, am Informationsschalter zu fragen.
3. Frage, von welchem Gleis der Zug abfährt.
4. Sage, dass man jeden Zug nehmen kann, aber in Bonn umsteigen muss.
5. Sage, dass man auf Taschendiebe aufpassen soll.

14 ... **scan a text for information**

a. Quickly scan the text for these dates. Note one thing that happened in each year.

1491 — Henry VIII was born
1502 — his brother Arthur died
1509 — he was the new king / his father died
1533 — he get married with his second wife
1536 — Anne Boleyn lost her head
1547 — Henry VIII died

b. Find all the girls' names. List them under *Henry VIII's wives and daughters* in your exercise book. Write a note about each woman or girl.

Catherine of Aragon:
- *wife of Arthur*
- *daughter (Queen Mary)*

Anne Boleyn:
- *daughter (Queen Elizabeth I)*

Jane Seymour:
- *(→Son: Edward)*

Anne of Cleves: (.....)
Catherine Howard (.....)
Catherine Parr: *still alive when Henry VIII died*

Henry VIII, the second son of King Henry VII, was born in 1491. His older brother, Arthur, died in 1502, and when his father died in 1509, Henry was the new king. He then got married to Arthur's wife, Catherine of Aragon.

In the early years, people loved Henry. He was clever, and he was famous all over Europe. But he had a problem. He needed a son to be England's next king. But Catherine only gave him daughters – and they almost all died. (Only Mary, later Queen Mary, lived.)

So Henry decided to get divorced, but this was very difficult at that time, and a lot of people were against it. But then in 1533 it happened. Henry got married to his second wife, Anne Boleyn, at once. But she too could only give Henry a daughter – the future Queen Elizabeth I.

This was not good enough for Henry, and by now he was getting old and horrible: in 1536, poor Anne lost her head.

In 1537 Henry's next wife, Jane Seymour, had a son – and died. Edward was not a strong child, so Henry got married again ... and again ... and again. He and Anne of Cleves got married in 1540 and got divorced weeks later.

In 1542 Catherine Howard came to the same end as Anne Boleyn. Catherine Parr was the lucky one. She and Henry got married in 1543, and she was still alive when he died in 1547.

When the Romans Ruled Britannia 3

1 Revision: It is, isn't it?
Complete the questions with question tags.

1 This comb is old, _____?
2 It isn't very valuable, _____?
3 You find lots like this, _____?
4 You can't say how old it is, _____?
5 It looks pretty, _____?
6 It was made by the Romans, _____?
7 You don't want it for the museum, _____?
8 Your expert looked at it yesterday, _____?
9 I'm allowed to take the comb with me, _____?
10 It doesn't cost anything, _____?

2 Which one?
Complete the sentences. Use a/the … one(s), this one or that one. The words in brackets will help you.

1 John likes new houses, but his parents live in (old) _an old ones_.
2 Which tile do you mean? (blue) _The blue one_ or (grey) _grey one_?
3 Mark thinks his mum's got a boring job, not (interesting) _not an intresting one_.
4 The archaeologists found two graves, (big) _a big ones_ and (little) _a little ones_. (big) _The big one_ is over there near the fence.
5 When you work with archaeologists, put some old clothes on, not (new) _new ones_.
6 These old coins are not very valuable. The Roman coins are (valuable) _valuable ones_.
7 That board game looks difficult, but _this one_ doesn't.
8 This amphora is older than _the other ones_.

3 Revision: If and when
Zak is thinking about his next History test. His last one was terrible. Put in *if* or *when*.

_____ I work hard now, I'll know more in the test. _____ I see the questions, I'll think about them first. _____ I think for a bit, my answers might be better. _____ I write more slowly, my answers will be tidier. _____ our teacher says stop, I'll put down my pen. _____ I get my paper back, perhaps I'll have an 'A'. _____ I get an 'A', Mum and Dad won't believe it!

TIP
Be careful with *wenn*! It isn't always 'when'. Wird es im Sinne von *falls* gebraucht, dann ist 'if' angebracht.

p. 41/A4

4 A boardgame
Complete the puzzle.

1. The Romans were in Britain from 43 … .
2. Archaeologists … up old things.
3. After their bath the Romans rubbed oils into their … .
4. There is often a … around a site to keep people away from it.
5. Someone who knows a lot about something.
6. Will you really take us to Bath? – Yes, I will. I … .
7. This gold chain is very … . It cost a lot of money.
8. The Roman …s fought against the Celtic tribes.
9. Britain was once part of the Roman … .
10. Another word for ketchup is tomato … .
11. The British 10 pence … has a lion on it.
12. We're cooking soup for 12 people so we need a big … .
13. The opposite of AD.

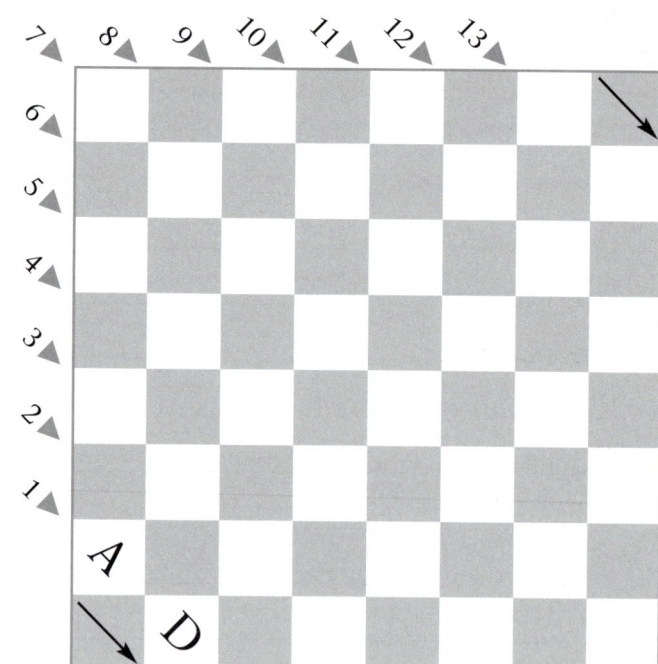

5 Revision: If we go to the Roman Painted House …
Fill in the right form of the verbs.

1. If you (want) __want__ to see the Roman Painted House, I (pay) __will pay__ for you.
2. If there (be) __are__ a lot of schoolchildren there, we (have to) __will have to__ wait a long time.
3. We (visit) __will visit__ another museum if we (have) __will have__ time.
4. If we (get) __get__ tickets for two museums, it (be) __will be__ cheaper.
5. If we (save) __save__ money with the cheaper tickets, I (buy) __will buy__ you an ice cream.
6. I (get) __will get__ that book about Roman Britain if you (want) __will want__.
7. If you (be) __are__ hungry later, we (go) __will go__ for some fish and chips – but without fish sauce or olive oil.

6 Word building

In Units 2 and 3 you learned about the suffix -ness and the prefix un-. Which of these adjectives can take the prefix, the suffix, and both the prefix and the suffix? Use a dictionary to check which words can take both prefix and suffix at the same time. The first one has been done for you.

adjective	un-	-ness	un- -ness
friendly	unfriendly	friendliness	unfriendliness
bright			
clever			
happy			
healthy			
lonely			
lucky			
tidy			

7 If I was in Rome ...

Complete the sentences below. The pictures and the clues in brackets will help you.
The first one has been done for you.

1. If I was in Rome, _my life would be easier_. (my life / easier)
2. If I lived in Spain, _I would go swimming in the sea_. (go swimming / sea)
3. If I worked here as a soldier, _I would often get wet_. (often / get wet)
4. If I was back in Rome, _could drink wine more often_. (can drink / wine / more often)
5. If I didn't live here, _could watch more exiting games_. (can watch / more / exciting games)
6. If I was living in Italy, _I would eat lots of spaghetti_. (eat / lots of / spaghetti)

3

8 I'd stay at the mansio in Dover ...
Imagine that you are a Roman who is talking to a friend who wants to go to Dover. Tell him where you would stay if you went there. Page 43 of your pupil's book and the clues next to this text will help you.

1. I would stay at the *mansio* if __I get good night's sleep__. *(get a good night's sleep)*
2. If you stayed there, you __would get good night's sleep__. *(get a good night's sleep)*
3. They have central heating there, so you would be comfortable even if _____.
4. It has 96 rooms, so if you went with some friends, there __will be enough space__. *(enough space)*
5. They have good Roman food there, so you would enjoy your meals if _____. *(in the mansio)*
6. And there are paintings of the gods on the walls, so if you chose the *mansio* I'm sure you _____. *(be pleased with your room)*

9 Mediation: If ...
You and a German friend are visiting an English family, the Millers. The father is an archaeologist. Your friend Julia doesn't speak much English. Help her.

Julia Können wir morgen die römische Ausgrabungsstätte besuchen, wenn es nicht regnet?

You Julia wants to know – *can we visit the Roman site tomorrow* __if it doesn't rain__?

Father Well, I don't know if she'll like it. If you're not an expert, perhaps it won't be very interesting.

You Mr Miller meint, wenn man __kein Experte ist kann es sein das es uninteresant ist und das er nicht weiß ob es ihr gefällt__

Julia Wer weiß? Es wäre sehr aufregend, wenn wir etwas Römisches finden würden.

You Julia says it __could be very exciting if we find something roman__.

Father Of course, but you'd only find something interesting if you looked for a long time.

You Er sagt, man __findet nur etwas spannendes wenn man lange Zeit sucht__.

Julia O.K., aber wenn wir es nicht probieren, entdecken wir nie etwas.

You Julia thinks that if __we don't try, we will never find sth.__

Father She's right. And have you decided what you are going to do if the weather is bad tomorrow?

You Er fragt uns, ob wir schon beschlossen haben, was __wir bei dem schlechten wie morgen machen werden__.

Julia Wir könnten ins Museum gehen.

You She says we __could go to the museum__.

p. 44/A11

3

Working with the text "Invaders"

Roman Baths and Pump Room
Pump Room, Abbey Churchyard, Bath
Telephone (01225) 477785
Opening hours Daily Jan-Feb 9.30am-4.30pm, Mar-Jun 9am-5pm, July-Aug 9am-9pm, Sept-Oct 9am-5pm, Nov-Dec 9.30am-4.30pm Last exit one hour after closing, Closed 25/26 December
Disabled access to Terrace only

The Roman bathing establishment with its magnificent Temple and Baths flourished in Aquae Sulis between the first and fifth centuries AD. It was built around the natural hot spring which rises at 46°C. The remains are remarkably complete and among the finest in Europe. They include sculpture, coins, jewellery and the gilt bronze head of the goddess Sulis Minerva. Free personal audio guides in seven languages are included in the tour. To complete your day, taste the waters and enjoy coffee, lunch or tea in the 18th century Pump Room above the Temple.

10 *Information from a tourist brochure*
Some German friends are planning a visit to the Roman baths in Bath in August. You've got a brochure from the Bath tourist office. Read the brochure and answer your friends' questions. Don't worry. To understand the text, you don't need to know all the words in the text!

1   Wann haben die *Roman Baths* offen? _____
2   Wie viel kostet der Eintritt? _____
3   Gibt es eine Führung? _____
4   Wie viel kosten die Audioguides? _____
5   Wie alt sind die *Roman Baths*? _____
6   Kann man dort auch etwas zum Essen und Trinken bekommen? _____

11 *Word detective*
English has a lot of words from other languages, e.g. Latin and French, but also from Scandinavian (Old Norse) and even a few from Celtic.

Try to be a word detective: listen to the CD and tick the right box for each word or place name. Don't forget to spot the words from Old English, too. PS: It's more fun if you don't look in your book.

Word	Celtic	Latin	Old English	Old Norse	French
blue	☐	☐	☐	☐	☐
Dover	☐	☐	☐	☐	☐
for	☐	☐	☐	☐	☐
lesson	☐	☐	☐	☐	☐
sky	☐	☐	☐	☐	☐
Thames	☐	☐	☐	☐	☐
the	☐	☐	☐	☐	☐
they	☐	☐	☐	☐	☐
wall	☐	☐	☐	☐	☐
wine	☐	☐	☐	☐	☐

pp. 49–52

3 TOPIC

12 Revision: So many questions!

Lavinia and Quintus have a lot of questions for Oliver and Chrissie. Answer their questions using relative clauses. Leave out *that* wherever possible. The words in the box will help you.

> ~~cart~~ • cheese • from London to Rome • ground • in oil • made from • ~~move~~
> olives • oven • potato • red fruit • to cook • to grow • to need • tomatoes
> warm countries • when you leave the country • ~~without horses~~

Lavinia   What's a car?

Oliver   A car is a kind of *cart that moves without horses* _____.

Quintus   And a pizza?

Chrissie It's a type of food _____
_____.

Quintus   But what are tomatoes?

Chrissie Oh, they're a type of _____.

Lavinia   What's a plane?

Oliver   It's a flying machine _____.

Quintus   You were talking about chips. What are they?

Oliver   Oh, they're pieces of _____.

Lavinia   Sorry, but we don't know what potatoes are.

Chrissie Potatoes are vegetables _____.

Quintus   Are they like passports?

Chrissie No, passports are things _____.

pp. 54–55

NOW YOU CAN ... 3

13 **... tell someone a secret in English**
How do you say these things in English?

1. Du bist ziemlich sicher, dass dein(e) Freund(in) keine Pläne für das Wochenende hat, aber frage nach.

   Do you have ~~time~~ any plans for weekend

2. Sage, dass du etwas vorhast, aber es ist ein Geheimnis.

   I have something to do, but it's a secret.

3. Sage, dass du versprichst, niemandem davon zu erzählen.

   I ~~swear~~ promise, I will not tell anyone

4. Sage, dass deine Mutter heiratet.

   My mum is going to marry

5. Sage, dass dir der Gedanke nicht gefällt, so viele Leute kennen zu lernen.

   I don't like ~~the~~ the idea of, ~~so that I will met~~ meeting so many people

6. Sage, dass er/sie aufhören soll, sich darüber Sorgen zu machen.

   Stop, ~~to~~ worrying about it

14 **... write a story**
Look at the pictures and write the story in your exercise book. Before you start, make notes.

- Think about: WHO? WHAT? WHERE? WHEN? HOW? WHY?
- Think of an interesting start for your story.
- Don't forget to use time expressions (e.g. suddenly, at first, after that) and linking words (e.g. although, because, so).
- These words will help you: *Juwelier/Goldschmied* = jeweller; *Tor/Gatter* = gate.

Now you and a partner When you have finished, close your exercise book and tell your partner your story. Your partner may ask you one or two questions. Try to answer them.

REVISION (Units 1–3)

1 *Plans for a trip*
Lizzy and her friends are thinking about what they could do at the weekend. Complete their conversation with conditional sentences (types I and II).

Lizzy So … what are we going to do – and when? We've got training on Saturday and a maths test on Monday.

Tony Well, if we (not have to) **didn't have to** learn for the test, it (be) ~~will be~~ **would be** good to do something together on Sunday. But we've got to learn for the test, haven't we?

Zoe Well, perhaps we could go somewhere if we (miss) **missed** training.

Zak Yes, that's right. And I've got a great idea for a trip. If we (not go) **don't go** to training on Saturday, we can visit Summer Island.

Dave But how are we going to get there? If we (want) **wanted** to go to Summer Island we (need) ~~would need~~ **will need** a boat. A boat probably costs £60 for the weekend.

Susie We can get a boat if each of us (pay) ~~could pays~~ **pays** £10.

Lizzy If I (have) ~~would have~~ **had** £10, I (love) **would love** to go. But I haven't got *any* money!

2 *Lizzy's ghost story*
Finish Lizzy's ghost story about the island. Look carefully at the beginning of each sentence and decide whether the *active* or *passive* is needed.

- 1623 – pirates¹ – take – Lady Anna
- take her – to Summer Island
- the poor girl – hide – in a secret place
- not give – food or water
- Lord Muck's soldiers – discover – pirates
- Lady Anna – never – find
- can – sometimes – hear – voice – at night
- last year – tourists – hear – her song
- wake – by her?

Lord Muck's daughter, Lady Anna, **was taken by** _____. They _____.

The pirates _____. She _____. Lord Muck's soldiers _____. But Lady Anna _____. Her voice _____. Last year some tourists _____. _____. Do you think we _____?

¹pirate [ˈpaɪrət] *Pirat*

28

(Units 1–3) REVISION

3 *A Roman party*

The picture shows a party at Lavinia's house. Fill in the gaps with the correct form of the verbs given in brackets. Be careful with the tenses. You need both *active* and the *passive* tenses.

They (have) _____ a big party at Lavinia's house. They (celebrate) _____ _____ for many hours. The children (be invited) _____ , too. Last week Lavinia's father (pay) _____ singers and dancers to come to the party. Two men (do) _____ acrobatics¹ for the guests. The guests (lie) _____ on sofas. They (eat) _____ since the afternoon. The party (last) _____ until late into the night. At the end of the party everyone (be given) _____ a special cake which (be cooked) _____ in wine.

¹acrobatics [ˌækrəˈbætɪks] *Akrobatik*

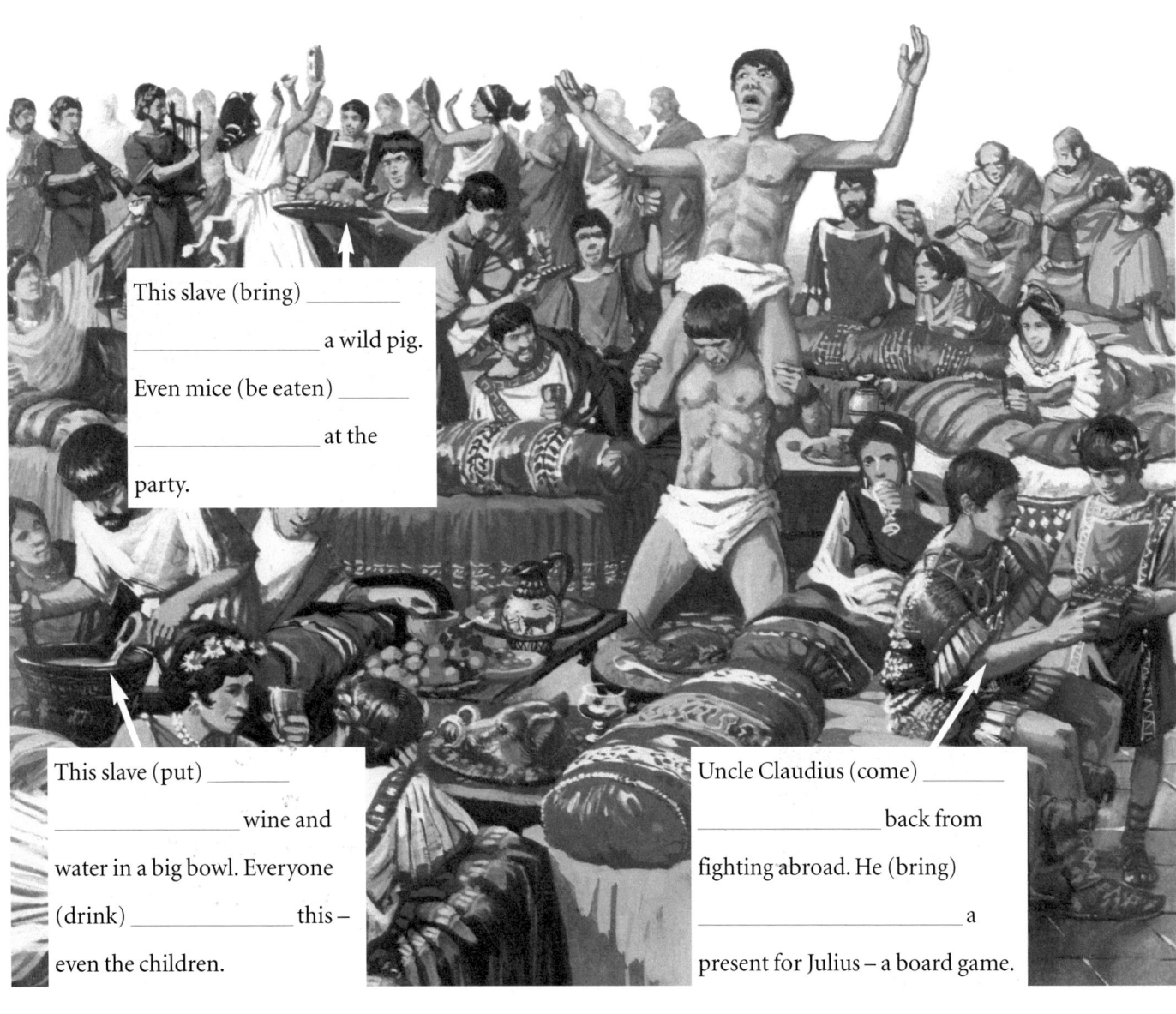

This slave (bring) _____ a wild pig. Even mice (be eaten) _____ at the party.

This slave (put) _____ wine and water in a big bowl. Everyone (drink) _____ this – even the children.

Uncle Claudius (come) _____ back from fighting abroad. He (bring) _____ a present for Julius – a board game.

4 Florida, Space and Sunshine State

1 American crosswords
Complete the crossword.

1. American money
2. The British write 'programme'.
3. The British say 'mark'.
4. Where the alligators are at home in Florida.
5. Americans who speak Spanish at home.
6. A party where you cook and eat outside.
7. You'll find one outside lots of US buildings.

Now you and a partner
Make your own crossword like the one below. Think of some words and write the clues. Let your partner complete your crossword.

1 _____
2 _____
3 _____

2 British and American English
These sentences were written by an American. The spelling of one word in each sentence is different in British English (BE). Underline that word. Then write it again with BE spelling.

TIP
If you need help with this exercise, look at page 161 at the back of your pupil's book.

1. I never go to the <u>theater</u>. — theatre
2. Who is your <u>favorite</u> singer? — favourite ✓
3. Pink is a nice <u>color</u>. — colour ✓
4. Do you say 'miles' or '<u>kilometers</u>'? — metres ✓
5. How far is it to the <u>center</u> of the city? — centre ✓
6. I <u>traveled</u> by plane. — travelled ✓
7. I'd love to see New York <u>harbor</u>. — harbour ✓

p. 59 (p. 161)

3 A postcard to a friend

Read the postcard on the right. Then imagine you are on holiday. Choose one of the other postcards and write it to a friend. Write

… where you are,
… what you're doing there,
… what the weather's like,
… what you're doing the next day.

Dear Jane,
Hi from the USA! I'm having a super time. This place is great. The course is a bit hard. But it's fun — much better than school. The weather is fine every day. I'm leaving tomorrow. My parents and I are going on a trip round Florida before we come home. Say hi to your mum.
Love, Margo
PS: Don't forget to send me a postcard.

To
Jane Harro..
43, Sulliva..
London SE ..
England

Dear Ricci,
I'm here in Florida, and it's just great. I'm at the beach right now and the sun shine's very bright and beatiful. Tomorrow I am going to go to an dolphin show and after I am going to swim with one of them. Hope you enjoy your holidays.
~~Dear~~ Love Charly ♥

4 Revision: Conchita and Margo

Complete this text about Conchita and Margo with the *simple past* or *present perfect*.

Conchita (meet) __met__ ✓ Margo the day before ATX. When she (go) __went__ ✓ to the hotel café all the tables (be) __were__ ✓ full, but a girl with red hair (ask) __asked__ ✓ her: 'Do you want to sit here with me?' It (be) __was__ ✓ Margo. 'Hi, I'm Margo,' the girl (say) __said__ ✓.

'Hi, I'm Conchita,' she (reply) __replied__ ✓ and (sit) __sat__ ✓ down. '(you/win) ~~Have you won~~ *Did you win* a day of ATX, too?'

'I (always/be) ~~was always~~ *have been* crazy about space,' Conchita (tell) __told__ ✓ Margo later.
'I (want) __wanted__ *have* to be an astronaut ever since I (be) __was__ ✓ a little girl. I (not believe) ~~san't believe~~ *didn't believe* it when I (win) __won__ a scholarship to ATX.'

'(you/visit) __Have you visited__ ✓ Orlando yet?' she (ask) __asked__ ✓ Margo.
'No, I (be) __was__ *have been* in Florida for a week, but I (not/see) ~~didn't seen~~ *haven't* Orlando yet,' Margo (tell) __told__ ✓ her. 'I want to go with my parents after ATX. Do you want to come, too?'

5 Timelines

Use the timelines below to complete the sentences about Conchita and Margo.
You need to use the *simple past*, the *past perfect simple* and the *past perfect progressive*.

1. When Conchita _came_ into the café, Margo _had been writing_ a postcard.

2. Conchita _____ Margo after she _____ from her hotel room.

3. Margo _____ a week in Florida with her parents before she _____ to ATX at Kennedy Space Center.

4. Conchita, Margo, Glenn and Scott _____ all a little sad at the end of the day because they _____ a great time on ATX.

5. Before Conchita, Margo, Glenn and Scott _____ , they _____ addresses and phone numbers.

6. Before the Blairs and Conchita _____ at Orlando, they _____ at a Mexican restaurant.

7. Conchita and Margo _____ all the time before they _____ to the restaurant.

Now you and a partner Draw three timelines of your own. Let your partner complete the sentences.

p. 60/A3

6 Telephone language

Sabine Müller is trying to ring her brother, Jan.
He is staying with an English family. Complete the dialogues.

Man	Hello?
Sabine	Oh, erm ... **Is there** 792356?
Man	No, it isn't.
Sabine	Oh, sorry. **I've got the wrong number**

Answer-phone	This is 792356. We can't answer the phone at the moment. **Leave a message** after the beep. Thanks.
Sabine	Oh nein, es ist der Anrufbeantworter!

Woman	Hello?
Sabine	Hello. **It's Sabine**. I'm Jan's sister. **Can I talk** to Jan, please?
Woman	I'm sorry, Jan's out. **Can I give him** a message?
Sabine	It's OK, thanks. **I call him later, again**

Later ...

Woman	Hello?
Sabine	Hello. Is Jan there, please?
Woman	**Who is there?**
Sabine	Oh sorry. It's Sabine, Jan's sister.
Woman	Oh, of course. **Hold on**. I'll get him.

7 My parents

Write about the things your parents let you do – and don't let you do. What do they make you do? What don't they make you do? The ideas in the box can help you.

- do jobs at home
- go to parties that finish late
- have parties when they're out
- pay for your own sports things
- choose the clothes you like
- take a friend on holiday
- go on holiday on your own
- ...

p. 61/A4 • p. 61/A6

4

8 Revision: What should they do?
Look at the pictures and write a sentence about each one using *modal auxiliary* verbs.

could • must (2×) • ~~mustn't~~ • needn't
not be allowed to • ought to • shouldn't

throw away / newspaper

pick up / rubbish

put on / pullover

write down / number

wake up / mum

cut out / photo

turn off / radio

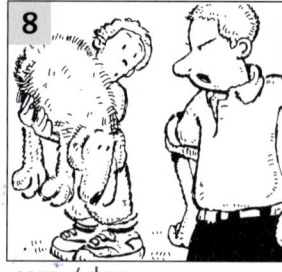
carry / dog

1 *She mustn't throw the newspaper away.*
2 _____
3 _____
4 _____
5 _____
6 _____
7 _____
8 _____

9 The Challenger tragedy
Complete the text with the verbs in the box.
Underline the verbs of perception.

~~appear~~ • ~~arrive~~ • ~~become~~
~~climb~~ • ~~count~~ • ~~happen~~ • ~~look~~
~~push~~ • ~~speak~~ • ~~stand~~

It was a cold morning in January 1986. At the Kennedy Space Center, a group of people stood together and <u>watched</u> the sun *appear* at last. I sat at my desk in the Center as usual. We were all waiting for something important. On my screen I <u>saw</u> seven people **arrive** in a large hall. They were ready for their mission. I <u>saw</u> the seven **stand** in front of the Challenger and **look** at it one last time. I <u>heard</u> nobody **speak** in the Space Center for a minute or two. Then the seven people were inside and we <u>listened</u> to the famous voice **count** the numbers: '10, 9, 8, 7, …'. I <u>felt</u> the whole Center **become** nervous in those last seconds. Then we <u>watched</u> the Challenger **climb** into the air. We <u>heard</u> the engines **push** it higher and higher, but 73 seconds later we <u>watched</u> a terrible tragedy **happen** in front of our eyes.

p. 61/A7 • p. 62/A9

10 Stressed syllables

Say these words. Where's the stress?
Put them into the correct list.

American • ~~astronaut~~ • attraction
community • except • exciting
explore • Hispanic • important • interested
menu • nervous • planet
prefer • programme • project • religion
restaurant • symbol • telephone

stress on the first syllable as in 'holiday'

astronaut	menu
symbol	intrested
project	nervous
program	restaurant
planet	telephone

stress on the second syllable as in 'vacation'

except	community
explore	important
Hispanic	exciting
American	religion
attraction	prefer

11 Mediation: At the fast food kiosk

An English tourist doesn't understand the menu at a German fast food kiosk. Help him to order.

Man — Was möchte er? Verstehst du ihn?
You — Can I help?
Tourist — Oh dear, I can't understand this menu.
You — Er sagt, dass er das Menü (Speisekarte) nicht versteht.

Man — Frag ihn, was er essen will.
You — What do you like to eat?
Tourist — I'd like something German. I can eat a hamburger at home.
You — Er mag etwas deutsches Essen, weil er Hamburger auch zuhause kriegt.
Man — Wie wäre es mit einer Currywurst?
You — Do you want a „Currywurst"?
Tourist — What's a 'Currywurst'?
You — It's a sausage with something kind a ketchup sauce and curry on it
Tourist — Fine. I'll have one of those and I'd like some chips, too, please. No salt.
You — Ok. Er möchte Currywurst mit Pommes aber ohne Salz.
Man — Alles klar. Das macht € 2,50.
You — Ok. That cost's 2,50€
Tourist — Great. Thanks for your help.

Haha, cool ♥
Charlotte
Theiss

4

Working with the text "Little Miss Astronaut"

12 *Practice with listening*

a Listening for stress: Listen to the CD. Where is the stress in the following words, on the first or the second syllable?

Underline the syllable which is stressed.

<u>cre</u> • dit   week • end

out • side   side • walk

b True or false? Listen again and tick the statements which are true. Put a cross next to the false ones.

1 After the trip to ATX, Conchita was too tired to tell everybody about the trip.
2 When Conchita went back to school, all the other kids wanted to hear about her trip.
3 Her teacher says the other kids are jealous because she has done something different.
4 When Conchita gave her talk about ATX, some kids didn't want to listen.
5 Most people in the class thought her talk was boring.
6 At the end of the story, Conchita is happy because she and Linda are friends again.

13 *Everybody's talking*

a After the Science class, everybody is talking about Conchita. Who might say these things?

1 Hey Rita, Conchita thinks she's so special. She thinks, 'I'm so great, and you guys are so ordinary.' You called her little Miss Astronaut too. And her talk was so boring. Why are you friends with her again? José is angry with you!

2 I think it's really great that Conchita won that scholarship to ATX. It was hard for her because some of the other kids in the class were horrible to her. She was sad at first, but I think she has learned something very important.

Person 1 might be _____.   Person 2 might be _____.

b Imagine you are Mike. What would you say?

_____
_____
_____
_____

pp. 68–70

TOPIC 4

14 *Mediation: Parents!*
You're on holiday with your parents in Florida. You've met two Americans and want to go swimming with them. But your parents have to agree. What would you say in English to your new American friends?

You	Darf ich mit Mark und Dolores schwimmen gehen?
Mother	Nein, darfst du nicht. Hier in Florida kann es gefährlich werden.
Dolores	What does your Mom say?
You	She says, no, I **can't be cause at the beach in Florida smt. dangerous can happen.**
Mark	What's dangerous about swimming on Cocoa Beach?
You	**Was ist so gefährlich wenn man am Cocoa Beach schwimmen geht?**
Father	Die Wellen sind sehr stark. Du könntest dich verletzen.
You	Dad says **the waves are very strong and I could hurt myself**
Mark	But we'll be with you all the time, and we know the beach.
You	Mark sagt, **das sie die ganze Zeit bei mir bleiben & das sie den Strand kennen.**
Mother	Musst du denn jetzt schwimmen gehen? Kannst du nicht bis morgen warten? Wir wollten in ein Café gehen.
Dolores	What's your Mom saying?
You	She says, **that they want to go to an cafe. And they ask if we can't wait till tomorrow so why we must swim today**
Mark	But we can only go swimming today. We have to go to school tomorrow.
You	Mark meint, **das wir nur heute schwimmen gehen können, weil sie morgen in die Schule müssen**
Father	Na, gut. Du kannst mit ihnen schwimmen gehen. Du brauchst nicht mit uns ins Café gehen.
Dolores	Well, can you?
You	Yes, he says **that I can go swimming and needn't go to the cafe.**
Mother	Ja, aber du darfst nicht zu weit schwimmen. Und du musst in zwei Stunden wieder hier sein.
You	She says I **must be here in two hours and I don't have to swim to far away**
Mark	Great! What are we waiting for?

pp. 72–73

4 NOW YOU CAN ...

15 ... do this crossword

1. a The American word for 'autumn'.
   b A very big room.
2. a You go here to get a plane.
   b When something is broken you need to ... it.
3. a 'My train arrives at 6 pm.'
      – 'OK. I'll come and ... you.'
   b The list of things you can eat in a restaurant
4. a You are ... when you are angry or unhappy because you want something somebody else has.
   b The AE word for 'pavement'.

```
        □ L L
        □ L L
      □ I R □ □
    □ □ I R
      □ M E □
      □ M E □
    □ □ A L □ □
  □ □ □ □ □ A L
```

16 ... write about someone you met

Think of an interesting person that you met somewhere. Perhaps you were on holiday, on a school trip, at a party, etc. The questions in the box can help you.

- Where did you meet this person?
- What did you like about him/her?
- What did you do together?
- Did you see him/her again after that?
- Did you write/phone?
- Why/Why not?

17 ... write a story about yourself

a Read this story about a day out.

It was a lovely warm day in June. I had a new bike and I wanted to try it, so my family and I went for a bike ride by a lake. We were having a great time, when suddenly the rain started. Everybody else jumped in their cars and left, but we had to wait under a tree. At last the rain stopped, but we were terribly wet.

b Read the story again and complete this table:

Where	by a lake
When	
Who	
What	
Why	

c Now write about a day when something (good or bad) happened to you. Fill in this table, then write the story in your exercise book.

Where	
When	
Who	
What	
Why	

Alaska – the Great Land 5

1 *Revision:*
Did you hear it happen?
Look at the picture on pages 74/75 of your pupil's book. What did you 'hear', 'see' and 'feel' on the imaginary journey to Alaska? Write sentences.
I could (not) hear / see / feel …

grasses • plane • school • tools • truck • wind woman • …

blow on my face
break under my feet
click • disappear • sing
start • take off • work • …

_____
_____
_____
_____
_____
_____

2 *Revision: Glen's ATX diary*
Complete the paragraph with verbs from the box.
Use the *simple past*.

be (3×) • build • go • have • look
(not) be • (not) fly • (not) get up
(not) like • wake up • watch • write

> **MONDAY**

I _____ at 7 o'clock, but I _____ until 7.30. I _____ breakfast in the café with the other kids in my team. The food _____ OK, but I _____ the bread. Scott and I _____ a bit late for training. The NASA astronaut _____ pleased! In the afternoon we _____ a fantastic spaceship. Well, it _____ great, but it _____ very well! The others _____ a movie in the evening, but I _____ to bed early and _____ a letter to my family. It _____ a good day.

Now you and a partner
Write your diary for one day last week. When you have finished, close your workbook and tell your partner what you have written. Your partner may ask you one or two questions. Try to answer them.

_____
_____
_____
_____
_____
_____

3 Revision: Glen's photo album

a Glen is showing a friend some photos. What is he saying? Use the *present perfect* and *since* or *for*.

1 We – live – Anchorage – 1997

   We have lived in _____ .

2 – father – work here – scientist – then.

   My father _____
   _____ .

3 Here's a picture of my mom. (– parents – be – divorced – more than five years)

   My parents _____ .

4 That's my sister Amy with her friend Judy. (– know – each other – they were kids)

   They _____ .

5 That's a girl I met at ATX. (– write – me two letters – I got back)

   She _____ .

b Now he's calling his mum on the phone. What is he saying? Use the *present perfect progressive*.

1 Amy is angry with me. We (fight) *have been fighting* _____ .

2 It's 8 o'clock and Dad still isn't home. He (work) _____ since 8 o'clock this morning.

3 I'm feeling tired. I (learn) _____ for a test.

4 Amy is stupid. She (try) _____ to learn Inupiaq for weeks.

4 Revision: Before ATX

Match the sentence halves. Then put the verbs in brackets in the *simple past* or the *past perfect*.

1 After Glen (see) _____ a TV programme about ATX,

2 Glen (not, talk) _____ to his dad about going to ATX

3 Glen (be) _____ really interested

4 After Glen (read) _____ about ATX scholarships,

5 When Glen (write) _____ his letter,

6 Glen (be) _____ a bit nervous before his trip to Florida

• until he (find) _____ some more information on the internet.

• because he (always, want) _____ _____ to travel.

• he (ask) _____ his teacher for more information.

• because he (never, travel) _____ _____ alone before.

• he (decide) _____ to write a letter and ask for one.

• he (wait) _____ nervously for the answer.

p. 76/A1

5 Going whaling

These are some of the questions about whaling which Amy asked people in Barrow. What does she say when she is telling a friend about it later? Use question words and the *to*-infinitive.

1 "When can I go whaling?"

 Grandma told me *when to go whaling*.

2 "Where do you find whales?"

 The man explained where to find whales.

3 "What should I take with me when I go whaling?"

 He gave me instructions about what to take with me.

4 "How can I make a good harpoon?"

 He told me how to make a good harpoon.

5 "Where can I put up the tent?"

 He showed me where to put the tent.

6 "How do you get the whale onto the ice?"

 The man described how to get the whale onto ice.

7 "When can I come whaling again?"

 He told me when to come whaling again.

6 Before Amy's trip

Look at what people said to Amy before her trip. Complete the sentences below.

1 — Barrow is a place that you can visit in the summer.
2 — Inupiaq is an easy language that you can learn quickly.
3 — The Whaling Festival is something that you should see while you're there.
4 — The museum is an interesting place that you can visit in Barrow.
5 — Will you find enough things that you can do in Barrow?
— I know the right man who can teach you to drive an ATV.
— What's the best place where you can go skiing?

1 Grandma said that Barrow was a place *to visit in the summer*.

 She said she knew the right man _____.

2 Dad told me that Inupiaq was an easy language _____.

3 Mom told me that the Whaling Festival was something _____.

 She also said the museum was an interesting place _____.

4 Glen asked what the best place was _____.

5 My friend Judy asked if I would find enough things _____.

p. 76/A1

5

7 Mediation: A talk on whaling

Imagine your Science teacher has asked you and a partner to give a talk on whaling. You have found some information on the Internet – but it's in English. Complete the conversation. (Tip: Look at page 116 of your pupil's book for help.)

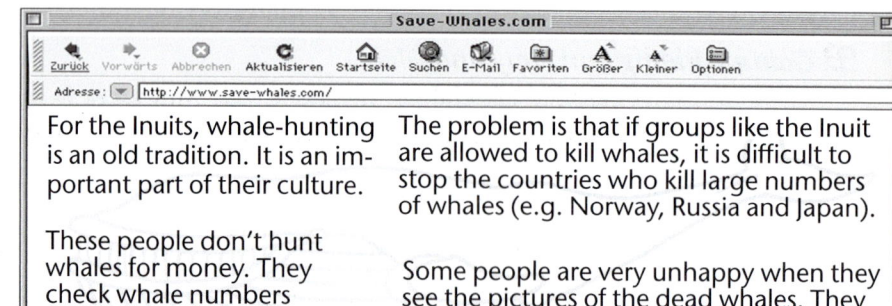

For the Inuits, whale-hunting is an old tradition. It is an important part of their culture.

These people don't hunt whales for money. They check whale numbers and are careful not to kill too many whales.

The problem is that if groups like the Inuit are allowed to kill whales, it is difficult to stop the countries who kill large numbers of whales (e.g. Norway, Russia and Japan).

Some people are very unhappy when they see the pictures of the dead whales. They say whaling belongs to the past. Today we should save the whales, not kill them.

Partner Wir brauchen einige Punkte *für* den Walfang. Seit wann machen das die Inuit?

You Also hier steht, dass es eine alte Tradition der Inuit ist Wale zu fangen und das es ein Teil ihrer Kultur is

Partner Okay. Dürfen sie so viele Wale töten, wie sie wollen?

You Hier steht noch, dass sie Wale nicht für Geld töten und immer auf ihre Bestände achten. Auch immer achten sie immer darauf nicht zu viele zu töten.

Partner Gut. Jetzt brauchen wir noch einige Punkte *gegen* den Walfang.

You Es ist schwirig andere Länder die Wale in großen Mengen zu töten zu stoppen. Außerdem gefallen den Leuten die Bilder des Walfangs nicht

Partner Steht da noch was?

You Ja, das zum Beispiel Russland, Norwegen und Japan die Länder sind die großen Walfang betreiben. Leute sagen der Walfang gehört in die Vergangenheit nicht in die Gegenwart.

8 The German word 'man'

Which words can you translate with 'man'? Circle them.

9 I'm worried about Amy and Glen

Grandma is telling Todd Oktollik on the phone what Amy wrote in her letter. Underline the reporting verb if it is in the *simple past* and complete the sentences. Page 77 of your pupil's book will help you.

Todd Hi Mom. How are things?

Grandma Fine, but I'm worried about Amy and Glen. I got a letter from Amy today and she said she __was arguing__ with Glen a lot. She thought that Glen __had changed__ since he'd come back from Florida.

Todd Yes, they've been having lots of arguments recently.

Grandma In her letter Amy said she __taught__ he __was__ jealous because she __had visited__ me last April. Anyway, I'm glad you told her she __could come__ here at Christmas. She wrote that she really __needed__ to practice her Inupiaq.

Todd I said she she __could come to__ you if she __could pay__ for half her flight.

Grandma That's right, but Amy's careful with her money, so that should be fine. Well, I hope that the two of them fight a bit less.

Todd So do I. At the moment they're fighting like two angry bears.

10 Dating in Barrow

After Glen talked to his father about Amy's visit to Barrow, he phones Amy to tell her about it (see pupil's book, page 78). Complete the sentences and change tenses, pronouns and adverbs where necessary.

Things are different in Barrow. Boys there aren't like the boys in Anchorage.

Dad said that things __in Barrow were different.__ __He said Boys there weren't like....__

When I was your age, we were all like the boys in Barrow today. The boys didn't ask the girls for a date. They would have been too embarrassed.

He said __when he was my age, they were all like.... today. The boys wouldn't ask..... They would have been too em...__

I wonder if Amy will like it in Barrow, because she'll find that a lot of things are different.

He wondered if __would like it...., would find that a lot of things were....__

And you're right – dating is much harder there.

We both agreed that dating __would be much harder there__

p. 78/A7

5

11 Nouns and verbs with the same form

a Underline the words in the box that are both *verbs* and *nouns*.

b Now look at the words you have underlined and complete each of these sentences with one of them. (You might have to change the form of the word if it is a verb.)

> answer • arrive • call
> celebrate • change • date
> design • destroy • dream
> fish • joke • point • report
> ride • show • sleep • sound
> stop • talk • visit • work

1 Glen has just written a *report* _____ on his _____ to ATX.
2 He is planning to _____ rockets when he is older.
3 Tomorrow he is giving a _____ about ATX at his school.
4 Glen always makes _____ about Inuit traditions.
5 Amy always _____ of going whaling.
6 When she was younger, her father taught her to _____ and hunt.
7 Whaling was different. It was very hard _____.
8 She'd like to live in Barrow, but it would be a big _____ for her.

12 Plurals

Write down the *plurals* of these words.
One word in each group has a different kind of plural. (Circle) it.

wolf _____	mouse _____	photo _____	fish _____
family _____	foot _____	life _____	city _____
thief _____	animal _____	guy _____	body _____
knife _____	tooth _____	valley _____	story _____

13 A quick note

Complete the text with the correct prepositions from the box.

> about • for • from • in
> of • on • to • with

Dear Ann,

Just a quick note to say hi! Today wasn't a great day. There are some horrible kids in my class. If you're not a member _____ their gang, they make fun _____ you. They wait _____ me and my friends after school. My brother says he'll protect me _____ them – ha, ha! He's always arguing _____ things with me. (Mom says he's jealous _____ me.) Oh well, I can't spend all my time _____ those stupid kids. I prefer _____ think _____ the vacation. I'm going _____ a trip next week and I want to be ready _____ it. I'm real excited[1] _____ it. Perhaps I'll meet someone nice and fall _____ love _____ him. I have to stop now and hunt _____ my bag.

Lots of love,

[1] real excited (AE infml) echt aufgeregt

p. 79/A10

Working with the text "Alone on the North Slope"

14 *Camping and hunting*

Complete the network with words from the text on pages 84–85 of your pupil's book. Add more lines and words if you can.

- CAMPING AND HUNTING
  - a fire
  - weather
  - to put up a
  - equipment
  - hunting
    - to hunt
  - animals
    - whale

15 *Practising listening*

a Which sound was it? Listen to the CD. Then tick the correct sound for the underlined word.

1 He knew he was a <u>dead</u> man. [ded] □ [di:d] □

2 If the cold didn't kill him, the <u>bears</u> would. [brəz] □ [beəz] □

3 As a boy he had <u>read</u> that the Inuit had melted snow … [ri:d] □ [red] □

4 He tried to <u>tear</u> off a piece of material from the tent … [teə] □ [tɪə] □

5 But what could he <u>use</u> to catch the rabbit? [ju:z] □ [ju:s] □

b Facts from the text. Listen to the CD again and answer the questions.

1 Why had Lester and Henry come to the North Slope?

2 What are Lester's and Henry's jobs?

3 How far was the nearest town?

4 What had Lester's grandfather told him about tools?

5 What were Lester's best tools?

5 TOPIC

16 *Mediation: A talk on Alaska*

You have joined an Internet chat room for Alaska fans. Recently you went to an interesting talk on Alaska. You have decided to send the others in the chat room the report on the talk in your local paper. Write the newspaper report in English.

Herr Blumenthal erklärte, dass die Russen die ersten Europäer in Alaska waren. Es gebe immer noch eine russische Kathedrale in Sitka, der alten Hauptstadt von Alaska.

Er fügte hinzu, dass der US-Politiker William Seward 1867 Alaska von den Russen für $7,2 Millionen gekauft habe. Viele hätten damals über „Sewards Eisschrank" gelacht, aber heute sei Alaska einer der reichsten Bundesstaaten der USA. Er erklärte, dass Alaska so reich geworden sei, weil der Bundesstaat viel Öl und Gas habe.

Er sprach jedoch auch von der Schattenseite des Öls: Nach einem Unfall im Jahre 1989 hätten mehr als 40 Millionen Liter Öl aus dem Supertanker Exxon Valdez die Küste Alaskas verschmutzt. Er erwähnte auch, dass das für die Tierwelt Alaskas eine schreckliche Tragödie wäre.

Aber es gebe nicht nur Schattenseiten: Alaska sei auch für den höchsten Berg Amerikas, Mount McKinley, berühmt, und für das Hundeschlittenrennen zwischen Nome und Anchorage, eine Entfernung von 1688 km!

NOW YOU CAN ... 5

17 **... be unhappy in English**
How do you say these things in English?

1 Ich bin erkältet.
_____

2 Ich friere!
_____

3 Ich sitze hier seit Stunden.
_____
_____

4 Ich glaube, die anderen machen sich über mich lustig.
_____
_____

5 Vielleicht wollen sie mir eine Lektion erteilen.
_____
_____

18 **... find the group words**
What are they?

1 Supper is a _____ .
2 A car is a _____ .
3 A wolf is a _____ .
4 A group of wolves is a _____ .
5 The Inuit are native _____ .

6 The USA is a _____ .
7 Alaska is a _____ .
8 Anchorage is a _____ .
9 The Mississippi is a _____ .
10 Denali is a _____
and a _____ .

19 **... write about the trip you'd like to go on**
Where would you like to go? The USA? Alaska perhaps? Or Florida?
Or would you prefer somewhere different? Write about your dream trip.

- Who would you take with you? Why?
- What would/wouldn't you do?
- What/Who would you take photos of?
- Who would you like to meet there?
- What souvenirs would you take home?

5 HOW TO USE YOUR GERMAN-ENGLISH DICTIONARY

1 Getting to know your dictionary

a Look at the first and last entries on the page. <u>Don't look at the rest of the page.</u> Do you think you'll find the words below on this page?

	yes	no
Henne		
Helm		
heftig		
herausstellen		
herab		

Look for the words on the page to check your answers.

b Find five words with *two* translations.

_____
_____
_____
_____
_____

---

heiter — 594

heiter cheerful; *Film, Geschichte o. Ä.* amusing; *Wetter, Tag* fine; *aus heiterem Himmel* übertragen out of the blue
Heiterkeit cheerfulness; *Belustigung* amusement
heizbar *Pool, Heckscheibe o. Ä.* heated
heizen 1 *Verb mit Obj* heat **2** *Verb ohne Obj* have* the heating on; *Slang: schnell fahren* put* one's foot down; *mit Gas/mit Öl/elektrisch ~* have* gas/oil-fired/electric heating; *mit Kohle ~* burn* coal
Heizkessel boiler; **Heizkörper** radiator; **Heizkraftwerk** thermal power station; **Heizmaterial** fuel; **Heizöl** fuel oil
Heizung heating; *Heizkörper* radiator
Held hero [ˈhɪərəʊ]
heldenhaft heroic [həˈrəʊɪk]
Heldentat heroic [həˈrəʊɪk] deed
Heldin heroine [ˈherəʊɪn]
helfen help; *jm. bei etwas ~* help sb. with sth.; *~ gegen Mittel o. Ä.* be* good for; *er weiß sich zu ~* he can manage *od.* cope; *es hilft nichts* it's no use [juːs]
Helfer(in) helper; *Mitarbeiter* assistant [əˈsɪstənt]
Helfershelfer(in) accomplice
hell 1 *Adj*; *Licht, Himmel, Zimmer* bright; *Farbe* light; *Kleidung* light-coloured; *Klang* clear; *übertragen: intelligent* bright; **helles Bier** *etwa* lager, *AE* beer; *es wird schon ~* it's getting light already; *ein heller Kopf sein* have* brains; *der helle Wahnsinn* absolute madness **2** *Adv*; *scheinen, brennen o. Ä.* brightly
hellblau light blue
hellblond very fair
hellhörig: *das Haus ist sehr ~* you can hear everything in this house; *er wurde ~* he pricked up his ears
Hellseher(in) clairvoyant [kleəˈvɔɪənt]
hellwach wide awake (*auch übertragen*)
Helm helmet
Hemd shirt; *Unterhemd* vest, *AE* undershirt
Hemisphäre hemisphere [ˈhemɪsfɪə]
hemmen *Bewegung, Lauf o. Ä.* check; *Fortschritt o. Ä.* hamper
Hemmschuh *umg. übertragen* obstacle, impediment (*für* to)
Hemmung inhibition; *moralische* scruple
hemmungslos 1 *Adj* uninhibited; *moralisch* unscrupulous **2** *Adv* uninhibitedly; *~ weinen* cry uninhibitedly
Hengst stallion
Henkel handle
Henker executioner
Henne hen

her *hierher* here; *~ damit!* give me that!; *vom Inhalt o. Ä. ~* as far as the content *o. Ä.* is concerned
♦ *her sein*: *das ist lange her* that *was* a long time ago
herab down; *die Leiter ~* down the ladder
herablassen: *sich dazu ~, etwas zu tun* condescend [kɒndɪˈsend] to do sth.
herablassend 1 *Adj* condescending [kɒndɪˈsendɪŋ] **2** *Adv* condescendingly; *jn. ~ behandeln* treat sb. condescendingly
herabsehen übertragen: *~ auf* look down on
herabsetzen reduce; *übertragen* disparage
herangehen: *~ an* go* up to; *übertragen: Aufgabe, Problem o. Ä.* set* about; *wir sind falsch an die Sache herangegangen* we went about it in the wrong way
herankommen: *~ an mit der Hand* be* able to reach; *bekommen* get* hold of; *übertragen: leistungsmäßig* be* able to compare with
heranwachsen grow* up (*zu* into)
Heranwachsende(r) adolescent [ædəˈlesnt]
herauf up; *die Leiter ~* up the ladder
heraufbeschwören call up; *verursachen* cause, provoke
heraus out; *zum Fenster ~* out of the window; *aus Verzweiflung/Wut ~* in desperation/anger; *~ mit der Sprache!* out with it!
herausbekommen get* out; *Geld* get* back; *Geheimnis* find* out; *Lösung* work out
herausbringen bring* out (*auch Produkt, Buch o. Ä.*); *Theaterstück* stage; *er konnte kein Wort ~* he couldn't say a word
herausfinden 1 *Verb mit Obj*; *Lösung o. Ä.* find*; *übertragen* find* out, discover **2** *Verb ohne Obj* find* one's way out
Herausforderer, Herausforderin challenger
herausfordern challenge; *provozieren* provoke
Herausforderung challenge; *Provokation* provocation
herausgeben zurückgeben give* back; *ausliefern* give* up; *Buch, Zeitung* publish; *als Bearbeiter* edit; *Vorschriften* issue [ˈɪʃuː]; *jm. drei Euros ~* Wechselgeld give* sb. three euros change; *jm. auf zwanzig Euro ~* give* sb. change for twenty euros
Herausgeber(in) publisher; *Bearbeiter* editor
herauskommen come* out; *von Buch auch* be* published; *von Briefmarken*

---

from: *English G 2000 Wörterbuch* © Cornelsen/Langenscheidt 2002

2 Symbols and abbreviations

Find these short forms and symbols on the dictionary page. Then match them to the correct long forms.

- o.Ä. → = adverb
- jm. = American English
- jn. = adjective
- sb. = irregular form
- Adv = jemandem
- AE = jemanden
- sth. = somebody
- * = something
- Adj = oder Ähnliches

3 Dictionary practice

Look up the German words and correct the mistakes.

1 *We had a ~~hot~~ discussion. I got very angry.*

   hier: heiß = _____

2 *The weather was ~~cheerful~~ yesterday.*

   hier: heiter = _____

3 *You should ~~put down~~ your prices.*

   hier: herabsetzen = _____

4 *She has got ~~bright~~ hair.*   hier: hell = _____

5 *I can ~~get~~ the top shelf.*

   hier: herankommen an = _____

Dreamland California 6

1 The Golden Gate Bridge
Complete the crossword.

1. When the Forty-Niners left, Bodie became a … town.
2. The British say 'film', the Americans say '…'.
3. What's the fourth word? hot – cold   warm – …
4. In 1848 the … Rush started in California.
5. Cars, buses and lorries are all … .
6. Bodie was a gold-… town.
7. The designer of the Golden Gate Bridge came from … .
8. The ground is shaking – it's an … .
9. A man who acts in a play or film.
10. What's the … today? – It's 30°C.
11. You use a search engine to find something on the … .
12. A hot, dry area.
13. The place where they make films.
14. A word which means 'famous person' or 'very old story which may or may not be true'.
15. You write '25°C'. You say '25 … Celsius'.
16. What's the fourth word? live – life   die – …

2 Revision: Questions, questions
You 'meet' an Italian boy in a chat room. His family has just moved to California. Write these questions to him.

1. When – move – America?

2. Why – leave Italy?

3. like California?

4. What Italian things – miss?

5. visit Italy sometimes?

6. Have – brothers and sisters?

7. speak English or Italian – home?

8. go – American school?

p. 93/A4

6

3 Which is correct?
Underline the correct form in the sentences below.

1. Spider Man and Green Goblin are fighting *each other / themselves*.
2. To keep *each other / themselves* cool in the desert they drank lots of water.
3. The two boys started to call *each other / themselves* names and then they hit *each other / themselves*.
4. Kids, it's much harder to laugh at *each other / yourselves* than at other people.
5. Mr Brown and Mr Blair are talking to *each other / themselves*. They never talk to *each other / themselves*, not even to say 'hello'.
6. They smiled at *each other / themselves* when they heard that their movie had been a big success.

4 Revision: Add words
Use the symbols ✶ and ◊ to show where you could put the words on the left in the sentences on the right. (Sometimes there is more than one possibility.)

1. probably ✶   She'll be here on Saturday afternoon .
2. at about 3 pm ✶   I'll meet her at the station .
3. usually ✶   The train is late .
4. always ✶   It will be the same .
5. a bit ✶ ; sometimes ◊   I get bored .
6. quite ✶ ; really ◊   But it's nice .

5 Lots of questions!
Jerry and Suzy stayed with the Truongs for a few days. They were very interested in their life in the US and asked lots of questions. Mrs Truong told her neighbor later about their visit. This is what she said:

What's Tet?
When do you celebrate Tet?
Do you celebrate Christmas?
Why do Vietnamese people put money into red envelopes?

"Yes, we liked them a lot, but they asked lots of questions!

Jerry asked _____

And he wanted to know _____

Jerry wondered _____

He wanted to know _____
_____

How do you make banh chung pastries?
What are they like?
Are most Vietnamese here Buddhists?

Suzy wanted to know _____
_____

She asked _____

And Suzy asked _____ "

6 No funny tricks!

Todd is telling a friend how an exciting film on TV ended. What does he say? The original dialogue is given first.

> This is your last chance. Throw down the gun and come out with your hands up. Right, stand against the wall. Don't move. And don't try any funny tricks.

"It was very exciting.

The police officer said it _____

_____

He told him _____

Then he ordered _____

He told _____

And he warned _____ "

7 Mediation: Explaining traditions

Complete this conversation at the Tet Festival in San Francisco.

Tourist	Hast du eine Ahnung, worum es hier geht? Warum werden diese ganzen Knallkörper angezündet? Du sprichst doch Englisch. Frag doch mal den Mann da.
You	Excuse me, _____
Vietnamese	We always light them at Tet. They are against evil spirits.
You	_____
Tourist	Frag ihn, was für ein Fest sie gerade feiern.
You	_____
Vietnamese	It's the Vietnamese spring festival. It's called Tet.
You	_____
Vietnamese	You're from Germany, aren't you? What traditions do you have?
You	Er will wissen, _____
Tourist	Eine gute Frage …

Now you and a partner

Think of a tradition in your area. How would you explain it to a foreigner? Make notes first in your exercise book.
- Think about: WHO? WHAT? WHERE? WHEN? (WHY?)

When you are ready, explain your tradition to your partner.
Your partner may ask you one or two questions. Try to answer them.

6

Working with the text "Next Month ... Hollywood"

8 *Listening to the text*

a No stress with stress: Listen to the CD and mark the stress in the words. Underline the syllable which is stressed.

a • <u>round</u>   re • li • a • ble   ta • lent

out • fit   ac • ti • vi • ty   pre • sent (*vb*)

b Answer these questions on the text. You can listen again to the CD to help you.

1 What does Rodney want to be?

2 What did Ivy do at the talent night?

3 What happened when Ivy fell over a cable?

4 How did the audience react to this?

5 What did Ivy say about their act after the show?

9 *Guess what happened yesterday!*

Rodney often writes e-mails to his friends. Read through the text again and imagine what he wrote on the days these things happened.

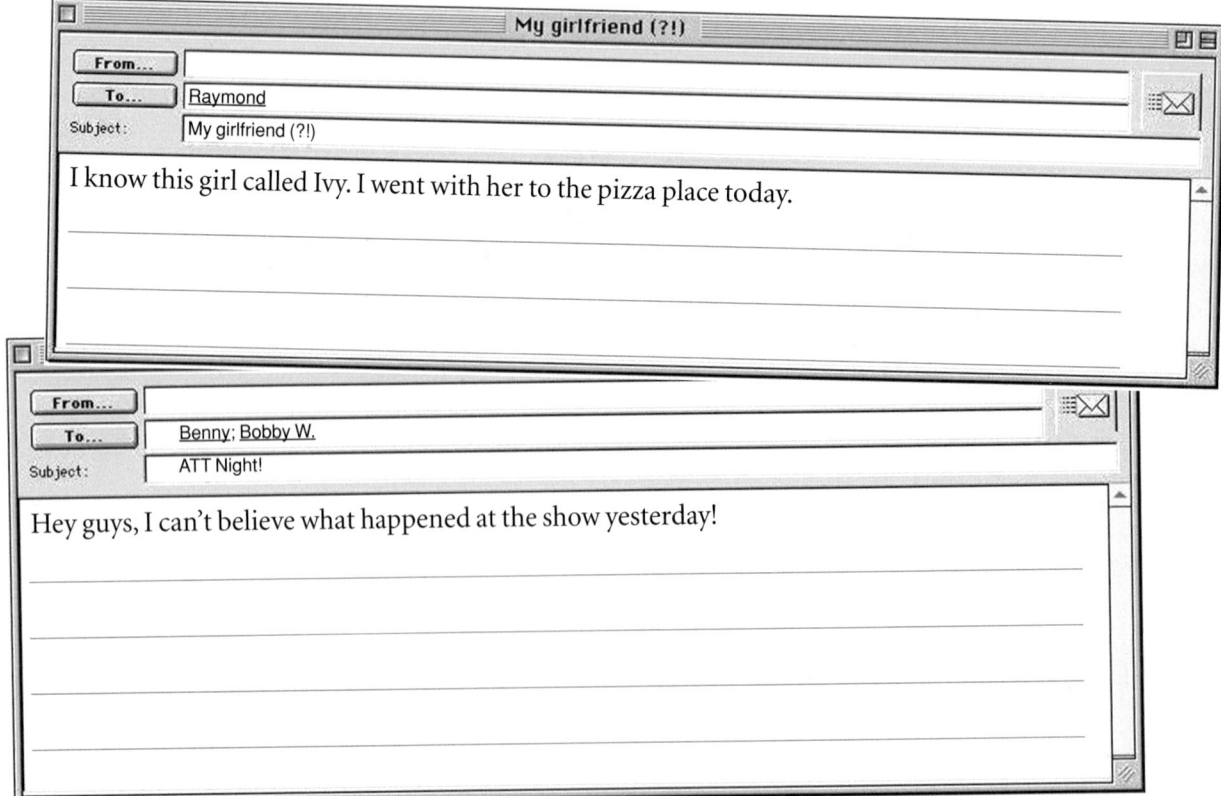

NOW YOU CAN ... 6

10 ... *talk about your dreams in English*
How do you say these things in English?

1 Ich bin verrückt nach alten Kinofilmen.

_____

2 Ich träume manchmal, dass ich Schauspieler/in bin.

_____

_____

3 Ich will viel Geld haben, wenn ich älter bin.

_____

4 Ich frage mich, ob ich es schaffen werde.

_____

5 Wird mein Traum wahr werden?

_____

11 ... *find the odd one out*
One word in each group is different. (Circle) it. Can you add any words to the groups?

bacon	record	desert	act
cookie	classical	coast	audience
bug	pop	valley	presenter
pastry	jazz	bridge	outfit
taco	rock	mountain	stage

12 ... *write for the school newspaper*
Have you seen a great film that you could tell other people about? Or heard a great song? Maybe you've seen a play or a concert? Or perhaps there's a great programme on TV that you think other people should watch? Write a short article like Julie's for the school newspaper.

> Last week I went to a talent show. Lots of kids from our school were in it. Everybody was really good, but the best act was Ice Happa (Rodney Suyama and Ivy Ramos). Rodney did a rap and Ivy walked up and down with a drum. The best bit was when they both landed on the floor. It was the funniest thing I have ever seen! You can see them at our school talent show this week. Don't miss it!
>
> *Julie Muramoto*

_____

_____

_____

_____

6 HOW TO USE YOUR ENGLISH-GERMAN DICTIONARY

1 Getting to know your dictionary

a Find the short forms of these grammar words on the page.

Adjektiv: _____

Adverb: _____

Plural: _____

Objekt: _____

b Find three grammar words that haven't got short forms.

_____

_____

_____

c Look at the phonetic symbols. Find one word for each symbol.

ɪ _____

aɪ _____

iː _____

θ _____

əʊ _____

d What's the adverb form of these adjectives?

She asked me (nice) _____ .

It's my turn (next) _____ .

e Find these short forms on the page. What do they mean?

AE _____

umg. _____

f What's the past participle of *nod*?

_____

---

from: *English G 2000 Wörterbuch* © Cornelsen/Langenscheidt 2002

2 Dictionary practice

Use your own dictionary and find the best German translation for the underlined words.

Fiorello Henry LaGuardia was a well-known[1] American politician in the 1930s and 1940s. He was raised[2] in Arizona, but moved to Italy as a young man. When he returned to the US he worked temporarily[3] on Ellis Island as an interpreter[4]. Later he entered politics[5] and in 1933 he was elected[6] mayor of New York City. He was very popular and for a long time he was the host[7] of his own radio programme. He did lots of good things for New York. For example, in 1936 he founded[8] the LaGuardia High School of Music and Art. Today New York's main airport is named after him[9].

1 _____ 6 _____

2 _____ 7 _____

3 _____ 8 _____

4 _____ 9 _____

5 _____

(Units 4–6) REVISION

1 *What happened first?*
Which of the two actions happened first? Write *1* for the first action and *2* for the second action.
Join the two sentences with *because*. Use the *past perfect* (*simple* or *progressive*) and the *simple past*.

They went to the Chinese restaurant without him.
He didn't want to join them.

They went to the Chinese restaurant without him because he hadn't wanted to join them.

We forgot to buy milk.
We went back to the shop.

I helped him to get up.
He fell downstairs.

It was raining in the morning.
I had my umbrella with me.

I went to the disco with my girlfriend.
I was sitting at home bored.

She didn't hear the phone at first.
She was listening to music.

2 *Glen would like me to visit him in Alaska*
Glen phoned Neil to invite him to come to Alaska.
This is what he said:

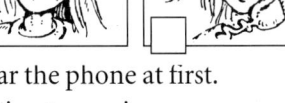

*Would you like to visit us in Alaska?
You could come next summer.
You'd need to ask your parents.
Could you please let me know soon?
It would be great if you could make it to Alaska.*

Now Neil is telling a friend about Glen's invitation:

Glen would like _____

He wants _____

Glen told _____

He wants _____

He would really like _____

55

REVISION (Units 4–6)

3 Mediation: What did you like most in the US?

A group of German tourists have been to different parts of the US. They are trying to talk to an American couple, Craig and Rita Willis, at the hotel about their trip, but are having difficulties with their English. Help them out.

Craig	What did you like most in the US?
Jürgen	Was hat er gefragt?
You	Er hat gefragt, was _____
Jürgen	Ach so. Ja, mir gefällt der Sequoia-Nationalpark hier in Kalifornien mit den riesigen Bäumen am besten. Ich habe nie gewusst, dass ein Baum so lange leben kann – 3000 Jahre!
Rita	What did he say?
You	He said _____
Beate	Für mich war es die Tierwelt Alaskas. Ich habe vorher noch nie Elche und Bären gesehen. Ich finde es nur traurig, dass es so viel Ölverschmutzung gibt. Warum kann man nicht mehr tun, um die Umwelt zu schützen? Das Land ist so wunderschön.
You	She said _____
	But she also said that _____
	She asked _____
	She added that _____
Oliver	Ich finde, dass das Raumfahrtzentrum in Florida interessanter ist. Warum soll ich nach Alaska fahren, um Bären und Elche zu sehen? Die kann man in einem Zoo sehen. Wir haben uns da gut amüsiert. Und die Tacos in Florida waren lecker!
You	*Oliver thought* _____
	He asked _____
	He said _____
	He said _____
Anna	Mir hat Hollywood am besten gefallen. Aber welche Tipps würden Sie geben? Was sollten wir besuchen, wenn wir nächstes Mal in die USA kommen?
You	*Ann said* _____
	But she asked _____
	She wanted to know _____